UNITY FROM PROFICIENCY TO MASTERY

C# PROGRAMMING

Master C# with Unity

Patrick Felicia

Unity from Proficiency to Mastery

C# Programming

First published: October 2017

Published by Patrick Felicia

CREDITS

Author: Patrick Felicia

BOOKS FROM THE SAME AUTHOR

Unity 5 from Zero to Proficiency (Foundations)

In this book, you will become more comfortable with Unity's interface and its core features by creating a project that includes both an indoor and an outdoor environment. This book only covers drag and drop features, so that you are comfortable with Unity's interface before starting to code (in the next book). After completing this book, you will be able to create outdoors environments with terrains and include water, hills, valleys, sky-boxes, use built-in controllers (First- and Third-Person controllers) to walk around the 3D environment and also add and pilot a car and an aircraft.

Unity 5 from Zero to Proficiency (Beginner)

In this book, you will get started with coding using JavaScript. The book provides an introduction to coding for those with no previous programming experience, and it explains how to use JavaScript in order to create an interactive environment. Throughout the book, you will be creating a game, and also implementing the core mechanics through scripting. After completing this book you will be able to write code in JavaScript, understand and apply key programming principles, understand and avoid common coding mistakes, learn and apply best programming practices, and build solid programming skills.

Unity 5 from Zero to Proficiency (Intermediate)

In this book, you improve your coding skills and learn more programming concepts to add more activity to your game while optimizing your code. The book provides an introduction to coding in C# t. Throughout the book, you will be creating a game, and also implementing the core mechanics through scripting.

After completing this book you will be able to write code in C#, understand and apply Object-Oriented Programming techniques in C#, create and use your own classes, use Unity's Finite State Machines, and apply intermediate Artificial Intelligence.

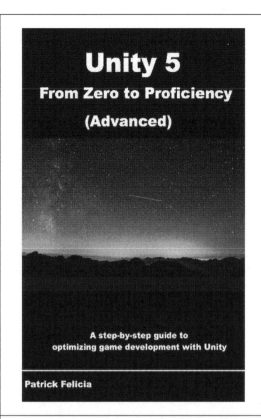

Unity 5 from Zero to Proficiency (Advanced)

In this book, which is the last in the series, you will go from Intermediate to Advanced and get to work on more specific topics to improve your games and their performances.

After completing this book, you will be able to create a (networked) multi-player game, access Databases from Unity, understand and apply key design, patterns for game development, use your time more efficiently to create games, structure and manage a Unity project efficiently, optimize game performances, optimize the structure of your game, and create levels procedurally.

A Beginner's Guide to 2D Platform Games with Unity

In this book, you will get started with creating a simple 2D platform game. The book provides an introduction to platform games , and it explains how to use C# in order to create an interactive environment.

A Beginner's Guide to 2D Shooter Games with Unity

In this book, you will get started with creating a simple 2D shooter game. The book provides an introduction to 2D shooter games, and it explains how to use C# in order to create an interactive environment

A Beginner's Guide to 2D Puzzle Games with Unity

In this book, you will get started with creating four different types of puzzle games. The book provides an introduction to 2D puzzle games , and it explains how to use C# in order to create four addictive types of puzzle games including: word games (i.e., hangman), memory game (i.e., simon game), card matching game, and a puzzle.

A Beginner's Guide to Web and Mobile Games with Unity

In this book, you will get started with exporting a simple infinite runner to the web and Android. The book provides an introduction to how to export and share your game with friends on the Web and on Android Play. It provides step-by-step instructions and explains how to easily share a simple game with your friends so that they can play it on your site or an Android device including: processing taps, exporting the game to a web page, debugging your app, signing your app, and much more.

ABOUT THE AUTHOR

Patrick Felicia is a <u>lecturer and researcher</u> at Waterford Institute of Technology, where he teaches and supervises undergraduate and postgraduate students. He obtained his MSc in Multimedia Technology in 2003 and his PhD in Computer Science in 2009, from University College Cork, Ireland. He has published several books and articles on the use of video games for educational purposes, including the Handbook of Research on Improving Learning and Motivation through Educational Games: Multidisciplinary Approaches (published by IGI), and Digital Games in Schools: a Handbook for Teachers, published by European Schoolnet. Patrick is also the Editor-in-chief of the <u>International Journal of Game-Based Learning (IJGBL),</u> and the Conference Director of the <u>Irish Conference on Game-Based Learning</u>, a popular conference on games and learning organized throughout Ireland.

FREE BOOK & VIDEOS

We all need some extra help and support now and then to keep motivated. So, as you subscribe to my list, you will be able to avail of the following for FREE:

- Access more than 20 video tutorials on Unity for FREE.

- Access an exclusive member area with plenty of resources.

- Receive weekly tips on game design and game programming.

- Gain access to a monthly giveaway where you can win some of my books on Unity and video courses for FREE.

- Get notified and receive my books weeks before they are published.

- Join a community of over 2000 subscribers and Unity fans who can help you when you need it.

- You can, of course, unsubscribe at any time, if you don't want to receive helpful and quality content anymore.

SUPPORT AND RESOURCES FOR THIS BOOK

You can download the resource pack for this book; it includes solutions scripts for some of the sections in this book, as well as some of the files needed to complete some of the activities presented in this book.

To download these resources, please do the following.

If you are already a member of my list, you can just go to the member area (**http://learntocreategames.com/member/**) using the usual password and you will gain access to all the resources for this book.

If you are not yet on my list, you can do the following:

- Open the following link: **http://learntocreategames.com/books/**

- Select this book ("**Unity from Proficiency to Mastery: C# Programming**").

- On the new page, click on the link labelled "**Book Files**", or scroll down to the bottom of the page.

- In the section called "**Download your Free Resource Pack**", enter your email address and your first name, and click on the button labeled "**Yes, I want to receive my bonus pack**".

- After a few seconds, you should receive a link to your free start-up pack.

- When you receive the link, you can download all the resources to your computer.

This book is dedicated to Helena

TABLE OF CONTENTS

PREFACE

After teaching Unity for over 5 years, I always thought it could be great to find a book that could get my students started with Unity in a few hours and that showed them how to master the core functionalities offered by this fantastic software.

Many of the books that I found were too short and did not provide enough details on the reasons behind the actions recommended and taken; other books were highly theoretical, and I found that they lacked practicality and that they would not get my students' full attention. In addition, I often found that game development may be preferred by those with a programming background, but that people with an Arts background, even if they wanted to know how to create games, often had to face the challenge of learning to code for the first time.

As a result, I started to consider a format that would cover both aspects: be approachable (even to the students with no programming background), keep students highly motivated and involved, using an interesting project, cover the core functionalities available in Unity to get started with game programming, provide answers to common questions, and also provide, if need be, a considerable amount of details for some topics.

I then created a book series entitled **Unity from Zero to Proficiency** that did just that. It gave readers the opportunity to discover Unity's core features, especially those that would make it possible to create an interesting 3D game rapidly. After reading this book series, many readers emailed me to let me know how the book series helped them; however, they also mentioned that they wanted to be able to delve into specific features in more details.

This is the reason why I created this new book series entitled **Unity from Proficiency to Mastery**; it is for people who would like to focus on a particular aspect of their game development with Unity.

In this book, focused on C# Programming, you will learn about C# concepts and how to use these in Unity.

CONTENT COVERED BY THIS BOOK

- Chapter 1, *Introduction to C# programming*, provides an introduction to C#, so that you become comfortable with C# programming and Object-Oriented concepts.

- Chapter 2, *Creating your First Script*, provides step-by-step instructions so that you can start creating your own scripts in Unity and implement some of the concepts introduced in the first chapter. You will also learn best coding practices, as well as how to debug your code and make it work smoothly.

- Chapter 3, *Introduction to Linear Algebra with C# for Unity*, provides an introduction to vectors; you will learn how to perform useful operations with vectors, and how these can be used in Unity and your games.

- Chapter 4, *Combining C# and Unity Objects*, provides practical explanations on using C# in your games. It identifies and illustrates some of the key (and frequently used) functions and classes that you would normally employ to create a game in Unity; both code snippets and in-depth explanations are provided. This section can also be used as a cook book, whereby you can go straight to the section that you need for your game.

- Chapter 5, *Optimizing The Structure and Efficiency of Your Code*, explains how it is possible to optimize your code and the overall structure of your game, so that your game is faster, more responsive (to provide a great user experience), and easy to maintain over time.

- Chapter 6 provides answers to Frequently Asked Questions (FAQs) related to the topics covered in this book.

- Chapter 7 summarizes the topics covered in this book and provides you with more information on the next steps to follow.

WHAT YOU NEED TO USE THIS BOOK

To complete the project presented in this book, you only need Unity 2017 (or a more recent version) and to also ensure that your computer and its operating system comply with Unity's requirements. Unity can be downloaded from the official website (http://www.unity3d.com/download), and before downloading it, you can check that your computer is up to scratch on the following page: http://www.unity3d.com/unity/system-requirements. At the time of writing this book, the following operating systems are supported by Unity for development: Windows XP (i.e., SP2+, 7 SP1+), Windows 8, and Mac OS X 10.6+. In terms of graphics card, most cards produced after 2004 should be suitable.

In terms of computer skills, all knowledge introduced in this book will assume no prior programming experience from the reader. So for now, you only need to be able to perform common computer tasks, such as downloading items, opening and saving files, be comfortable with dragging and dropping items and typing, and be relatively comfortable with Unity's interface.

So, if you would prefer to become more comfortable with Unity prior to starting this book, you can download the books in the series called Unity 5 From Zero to Proficiency (Foundations, Beginner, or Intermediate, Advanced). These books cover most of the shortcuts and views available in Unity, as well as how to perform common tasks in Unity, such as creating and transforming objects, importing assets, using navigation controllers, creating scripts or exporting the game for the web.

WHO THIS BOOK IS FOR

If you can answer **yes** to all these questions, then this book is for you:

1. Would you like to learn how to code in C#?

2. Would you like to know how to use C# to transform objects and to access their components?

3. Would you like to discover more C# features that you can use with Unity?

4. Although you may have had some prior exposure to Unity and coding, would you like to delve more into Object-Oriented Programming?

WHO THIS BOOK IS NOT FOR

If you can answer yes to all these questions, then this book is **not** for you:

1. Can you already create and optimize your own C# code in Unity?

2. Are you looking for a reference book on C# programming?

3. Are you a professional Unity developer?

If you can answer yes to all four questions, you may instead look for the other books in the series on the <u>official website (http://www.learntocreategames.com)</u>.

HOW YOU WILL LEARN FROM THIS BOOK

Because all students learn differently and have different expectations of a course, this book is designed to ensure that all readers find a learning mode that suits them. Therefore, it includes the following:

- A list of the learning objectives at the start of each chapter so that readers have a snapshot of the skills that will be covered.

- Each section includes an overview of the activities covered.

- Many of the activities are step-by-step, and learners are also given the opportunity to engage in deeper learning and problem-solving skills through the challenges offered at the end of each chapter.

- Each chapter ends-up with a quiz and challenges through which you can put your skills (and knowledge acquired) to the test. Challenges consist in coding, debugging, or creating new features based on the knowledge that you have acquired in the chapter.

- The book focuses on the core skills that you need. While some sections go into more detail, once concepts have been explained, links are provided to additional resources, where necessary.

- The code is introduced progressively and it is also explained in detail.

- You also gain access to several videos that help you along the way, especially for the most challenging topics.

FORMAT OF EACH CHAPTER AND WRITING CONVENTIONS

Throughout this book, and to make reading and learning easier, text formatting and icons will be used to highlight parts of the information provided and to make the book easy to read.

SPECIAL NOTES

Each chapter includes resource sections, so that you can further your understanding and mastery of Unity; these include:

- A quiz for each chapter: these quizzes usually include 10 questions that test your knowledge of the topics covered throughout the chapter. The solutions are provided on the companion website.

- A checklist: it consists of between 5 and 10 key concepts and skills that you need to be comfortable with before progressing to the next chapter.

- Challenges: each chapter includes a challenge section where you are asked to combine your skills to solve a particular problem.

Author's notes appear as described below:

Author's suggestions appear in this box.

Code appears as described below:

```
public int score;
public string playersName = "Sam";
```

Checklists that include the important points covered in the chapter appear as described below:

- Item1 for check list.

- Item2 for check list.

- Item3 for check list.

HOW CAN YOU LEARN BEST FROM THIS BOOK?

- **Talk to your friends about what you are doing.**

  We often think that we understand a topic until we have to explain it to friends and answer their questions. By explaining your different projects, what you just learned will become clearer to you.

- **Do the exercises.**

  All chapters include exercises that will help you to learn by doing. In other words, by completing these exercises, you will be able to better understand the topics and gain practical skills (i.e., rather than just reading).

- **Don't be afraid of making mistakes.**

  I usually tell my students that making mistakes is part of the learning process; the more mistakes you make and the more opportunities you have for learning. At the start, you may find the errors disconcerting, or you may find that Unity does not work as expected until you understand what went wrong.

- **Challenge yourself.**

  All chapters include a challenge section where you can decide to take on a particular challenge to improve your game or skills. These challenges are there for you to think creatively and to apply the knowledge that you have acquired in each chapter using a problem-based approach.

- **Learn in chunks.**

  It may be disconcerting to go through five or six chapters straight, as it may lower your motivation. Instead, give yourself enough time to learn, go at your own pace, and learn in small units (e.g., between 15 and 20 minutes per day). This will do at least two things for you: it will give your brain the time to "digest" the information that you have just learned, so that you can start fresh the following day. It will also make sure that you don't "burn-out" and that you keep your motivation levels high.

FEEDBACK

While I have done everything possible to produce a book of high quality and value, I always appreciate feedback from readers so that the book can be improved accordingly. If you would like to give feedback on this book, you can email me at learntocreategames@gmail.com.

IMPROVING THE BOOK

Although great care was taken in checking the content of this book, I am human, and some errors could remain in the book. As a result, it would be great if you could let me know of any issue or error you may have come across in this book, so that it can be solved and so that the book can be updated accordingly. To report an error, you can email me (learntocreategames@gmail.com) with the following information:

- Name of the book.

- The page or section where the error was detected.

- Describe the error and also what you think the correction should be.

Once your email is received, the error will be checked, and, in the case of a valid error, it will be corrected, and the book will be updated to reflect the changes accordingly.

SUPPORTING THE AUTHOR

A lot of work has gone into this book and it is the fruit of long hours of preparation, brainstorming, and finally writing. As a result, I would ask that you do not distribute any illegal copies of this book.

This means that if a friend wants a copy of this book, s/he will have to buy it through the official channels (i.e., through Amazon or the book's official website: **http://www.learntocreategames.com/books)**.

If some of your friends are interested in the book, you can refer them to the book's official website **(http://www.learntocreategames.com/books)** where they can either buy the book, or join the mailing list to be notified of future promotional offers or enter a monthly draw and be in for a chance to receive a free copy of the book.

1
INTRODUCTION TO C# PROGRAMMING

In this section, we will go through an introduction to C# programming and look at key aspects that you will need for your games, including:

- C# Syntax.

- Variable types and scope.

- Useful coding structures (e.g., loops or conditional statements).

- Object-Oriented Programing (OOP) principles.

So, after completing this chapter, you will be able to:

- Understand key concepts related to C# programming.

- Understand the concepts of variables and methods.

- Know how and why inheritance can be applied to your games.

The code solutions for this chapter are included in the **resource pack** that you can download by following the instructions included in the section entitled "**Support and Resources for this Book**".

INTRODUCTION

When you are using scripting in Unity, you are communicating with the Game Engine and asking it to perform actions. To communicate with the system, you are using a language or a set of words bound by a syntax that the computer and you know. This language consists of keywords, key phrases, and a syntax that ensures that the instructions are written and (more importantly) understood properly.

In computer science, this language needs to be exact, precise, unambiguous, and with a correct syntax. In other words, it needs to be **exact**.

When writing C# code, you will be following a syntax; this syntax will consist in a set of rules that will make it possible for you to communicate with Unity clearly and unambiguously. In addition to its syntax, C# also uses classes, and your C# scripts will, by default, be saved as classes.

In the next section, we will learn how to use this syntax. If you have already coded in JavaScript, some of the information provided in the rest of this chapter may look familiar and this prior exposure to JavaScript will definitely help you. This being said, UnityScript and C#, despite some relative similarities, are quite different in many aspects; for example, in C#, variables and functions are declared differently.

When scripting in C#, you will be using a specific syntax to communicate with Unity; this syntax will be made of sentences that will be used to convey information on what you would like the computer to do; these sentences or statements will include a combination of keywords, variables, methods, or events; and the next section will explain how you can confidently build these sentences together and consequently program in C#.

STATEMENTS

When you code in C#, you need to tell the system to execute your instructions (e.g., print information) using statements. A statement is literally an order or something that you ask the system to do. For example, in the next line of code, the statement will tell Unity to print a message in the **Console** window:

```
print ("Hello Word");
```

When writing statements, you will need to follow several rules, including the following:

- **The order of statements**: each statement is executed in the same order as it appears in the script. For example, in the next example, the code will print **hello**, then **world;** this is because the associated statements are in that particular sequence.

```
print ("hello");
print ("world");
```

- **Statements are separated by semi-colons** (i.e., semi-colon at the end of each statement).

> Note that several statements can be added on the same line, as long as they are separated by a semi-colon.

- For example, the next line of code has a correct syntax, as all of its statements are separated by a semi-colon.

```
print("hello");print ("world");
```

- **Multiple spaces are ignored for statements**; however, it is good practice to add spaces around the operators +, -, /, or % for clarity. For example, in the next code snippet, we say that **a** is equal to **b**. You may notice that spaces have been included both before and after the operator =.

```
a = b;
```

- **Statements to be executed together (e.g., based on the same condition) can be grouped using code blocks.** In C#, code blocks are symbolized by curly brackets (e.g., { or }). So, in other words, if you needed to group several statements, you would include all of them within the same set of curly brackets, as follows:

```
{

    print ("hello stranger!");

    print ("today, we will learn about scripting");

}
```

As we have seen earlier, a statement usually employs or starts with a **keyword** (i.e., a word that the computer knows). Each of these keywords has a specific purpose, and common keywords, at this stage, could be used for the following actions:

- Printing a message in the **Console** window: the keyword is **print**.

- Declaring a variable: the keyword, in this case, depends on the type of the variable that is declared (e.g., **int** for integers, **string** for text, or **bool** for Boolean variables), and we will see more about these in the next sections.

- Declaring a method: the keyword to be used depends on the type of the data returned by the method. For example, in C#, the name of a method is preceded by the keyword **int** when the method returns an **integer**; it is preceded by the keyword **string** when the method returns a **string**, or by the keyword **void** when the method does not return any information.

> What is called a **method** in C# is what used to be called a function in UnityScript; these terms (i.e., function and method) differ in at least two ways: in C# you need to specify the type of the data returned by this method, and the keyword **function** is not used anymore in C# for this purpose. We will see more about methods in the next sections.

- Marking a block of instructions to be executed based on a condition: the keywords are **if** and **else**.

- Exiting a function: the keyword is **return**.

COMMENTS

In C# (similarly to JavaScript), you can use comments to explain your code and to make it more readable by others. This becomes important as the size of your code increases; and it is also important if you work in a team, so that other team members can understand your code and make amendments in the right places, if and when it is needed.

Code that is commented is usually not executed. There are two ways to comment your code in C# using either **single-** or **multi-line** comments.

In single-line comments, a **double forward slash** is added at the start of a line or after a statement, so that this line (or part thereof) is commented, as illustrated in the next code snippet.

```
//the next line prints Hello in the console window
print ("Hello");
//the next line declares the variable name
string name;
name = "Hello";//sets the value of the variable name
```

In multi-line comments, any code between the characters forward slash and star " /*" and the characters star and forward slash "*/" will be commented, and this code will not be executed. This is also referred as **comment blocks**.

```
/* the next lines after the comments will print the message
"hello" in the console window
we then declare the variable name and assign a value
*/
print("Hello");
string name;
name = "Hello";//sets the value of the variable name
//print ("Hello World")
/*
      string name;
      name = "My Name";
*/
```

VARIABLES

A variable can be compared to a container that includes a value that may change over time. When using variables, we usually need to: (1) declare the variable by specifying its type, (2) assign a value to this variable, and (3) possibly combine this variable with other variables using operators, as illustrated in the next code snippet.

```
int myAge;//we declare the variable myAge

myAge = 20;// we set the variable myAge to 20

myAge = myAge + 1; //we add 1 to the variable myAge
```

In the previous example, we have declared a variable called **myAge** and its type is **int** (as in **integer**). We save the value **20** in this variable, and we then add **1** to it.

Note that, contrary to UnityScript, where the keyword **var** is used to declare a variable, in C# the variable is declared using its type followed by its name. As we will see later, we will also need to use what is called an **access modifier** in order to specify how and from where this variable can be accessed.

Also note that in the previous code, we have assigned the value **myAge + 1** to the variable **myAge**; the = operator is an assignment operator; in other words, it is there to assign a value to a variable and is not to be understood in a strict algebraic sense (i.e., that the values or variables on both sides of the = sign are equal).

To make C# coding easier and leaner, you can declare several variables of the same type in one statement. For example, in the next code snippet, we declare three variables **v1**, **v2**, and **v3** in one statement. This is because they are of the same type (i.e., they are **integers**).

```
int v1,v2,v3;
int v4=4, v5=5, v6=6;
```

In the code above, the first line declares the variables **v1**, **v2**, and **v3**. All three variables are **integers**. In the second line of code, not only do we declare three variables simultaneously, but we also initialize them by setting a value for each of these variables.

When using variables, there are a few things that we need to determine including their name, their type and their scope:

- **Name of a variable:** a variable is usually given a unique name so that it can be identified easily and uniquely. The name of a variable is usually referred to as an **identifier**. When defining an identifier, it can contain letters, digits, a minus, an underscore or a dollar sign, and it usually begins with a letter. Identifiers cannot be keywords, such as the keyword **if**, for example.

- **Type of variable:** variables can hold several types of data, including numbers (e.g., integers, doubles or floats), text (e.g., strings or characters), Boolean values (e.g., true or false), arrays, objects (we will see the concept of arrays later in this chapter) or **GameObjects** (i.e., any object included in your scene), as illustrated in the next code snippet.

```
string myName = "Patrick";//the text is declared using double
quotes

int currentYear = 2017;//the year needs no decimals and is
declared as an integer

float width = 100.45f;//the width is declared as a float (i.e.,
with decimals)
```

- **Variable declaration:** variables need to be declared so that the system knows what you are referring to if you use this variable in your code. The first step in using a variable is to declare or define this variable. At the declaration stage, the variable does not have to be assigned a value, as this can be done later. In the next example, we declare a variable called **myName** and then assign the value **"My Name"** to it.

```
string myName;
myName = "My Name"
```

- **Scope of a variable:** a variable can be accessed in specific contexts that depend on where in the script the variable was initially declared. We will look at this concept later.

- **Accessibility level:** as we will see later, a C# program consists of classes; for each of these classes, the methods and variables within can be accessed depending on their **accessibility** levels and we will look at this principle later.

Common variable types include:

- **String**: same as text.

- **Int**: integer (1, 2, 3, etc.).

- **Boolean**: true or false.

- **Float**: with a fractional value (e.g., 1.2f, 3.4f, etc.).

- **Arrays**: a group of variables of the same type. If this is unclear, not to worry, this concept will be explained further in this chapter.

- **GameObject**: a game object (any game object in your scene).

ARRAYS

You can optimize your code with arrays, as they make it easier to apply features and similar behaviors to a wide range of data. When you use arrays, you can manage to declare less variables (for variables storing the same type of information) and to also access them more easily. You can create either single-dimensional arrays or multi-dimensional arrays.

Let's look at the simplest form of arrays: **single-dimensional arrays**. For this concept, we can take the analogy of a group of 10 people who all have a name. If we wanted to store this information using a string variable, we would need to declare (and to set) ten different variables, as illustrated in the next code snippet.

```
string name1;string name2; ......
```

While this code is perfectly fine, it would be great to store this information in only one variable instead. For this purpose, we could use an array. An array is comparable to a list of items that we can access using an index. This index usually starts at 0 for the first element in the array.

So let's see how we store the names with an array.

- First we could declare the array as follows:

```
string [] names;
```

You will probably notice the syntax **dataType [] nameOfTheArray**. The opening and closing square brackets are used to specify that we declare an **array** that will include string values.

- Then we could initialize the array as follows:

```
names = new string [10];
```

In the previous code, we just specify that our new array, called **names**, will include 10 string variables.

- We can then store information in this array as described in the next code snippet.

```
names [0] = "Paul";
names [1] = "Mary";
...
names [9] = "Pat";
```

In the previous code, we store the name **Paul** as the first element in the array (remember the index starts at 0); we store the second element (with the index 1) as **Mary**, as well as the last element (with the index 9), **Pat**.

> Note that for an array of size **n, the index of the first element is 0** and **the index of the last element is n-1**. So for an array of size 10, the index for the first element is 0, and the index of the last element is 9 (i.e., 10-1).

If you were to use arrays of integers or floats, or any other type of data, the process would be similar, as illustrated in the next code snippet.

```
int [] arrayOfInts; arrayOfInts [0] = 1;
float [] arrayOfFloats;arrayOfLoats[0]=2.4f;
```

Now, one of the cool things that you can do with arrays is that you can initialize your array in one line, saving you the headaches of writing 10 lines of code if you have 10 items in your array, as illustrated in the next example.

```
string [] names = new string [10] {"Paul","Mary","John","Mark",
"Eva","Pat","Sinead","Elma","Flaithri", "Eleanor"};
```

This is very handy, as you will see in the next chapters, and this should definitely save you a lot of time coding.

Now that we have looked into single-dimensional arrays, let's look at multidimensional arrays, which can also be very useful when storing information. This type of array (i.e., multidimensional arrays) can be compared to a building with several floors, each with several apartments. So let's say that we would like to store the number of tenants for each apartment. We would, in this case, create variables that would store this number for each of these apartments.

The first solution would be to create variables that store the number of tenants for each of these apartments with a variable that makes a reference to the floor, and the number of the apartment. For example, the variable **ap0_1** could be defined to store the number of tenants in the first apartment on the ground floor, **ap0_2**, could be defined to store the number of tenants in the second apartment on the ground floor, **ap1_1** could be defined to store the number of tenants in the second apartment on the first floor, and **ap1_2**, could be defined to store the number of tenants in the third apartment on the first floor. So in term of coding, we could have the following:

```
int ap0_1 = 0;

int ap0_2 = 0;

...
```

However, we could also use arrays in this case, as illustrated in the next code snippet:

```
int [,] apArray = new int [10,10];

apArray [0,1] = 0;

apArray [0,2] = 0;

print (apArray[0]);
```

In the previous code:

- We declare our array. **int [,]** means a two-dimensional array with integers; in other words, we state that any element in this array will be defined and accessed based on two parameters: the floor level and the number of this apartment on that level.

- We also specify a size (or maximum) for each of these parameters. The maximum number of floors (or level) will be 10, and the maximum number of apartment per floor will be 10. So, for this example we can define levels, from level 0 to level 9 (i.e., 10 levels), and from apartment 0 to apartment 9 (i.e., 10 apartments).

- The last line of code prints the value of the first element of the array in the **Console** window.

One of the other interesting things with arrays is that, by using a loop, you can write a single line of code to access all the items in this array, and hence, write more efficient code.

CONSTANTS

So far we have looked at variables and how you can store and access them seamlessly in your code. The assumption then was that a value may change over time, and that this value would be stored in a variable accordingly. However, there may be times when you know that a value will remain constant throughout your game. For example, you may want to define labels that refer to values that should not change over time, and in this case, you could use constants.

Let's see how this works: let's say that the player has three choices in the first menu of the game, that we will call 0, 1, and 2. Let's assume that you would like an easy way to remember these values so that you can process the corresponding choices. Let's look at the following code that illustrates this idea:

```
int userChoice = 2;
if (userChoice == 0) print ("you have decided to restart");
if (userChoice == 1) print ("you have decided to stop the game");
if (userChoice == 2) print ("you have decided to pause the game");
```

In the previous code:

- The variable **userChoice** is an integer and is set to **2**.

- We then check the value of the variable **userChoice** and print a message accordingly in the console window.

Now, as you add more code to your game, you may or may not remember that the value **0** corresponds to restarting the game; the same applies to the other two values defined previously. So instead, we could use constants to make it easier to remember (and to use) these values. Let's see how the previous example can be modified to employ constants instead.

```
const int CHOICE_RESTART = 0;

const int CHOICE_STOP = 1;

const int CHOICE_PAUSE = 2;

int userChoice = 2;

if (userChoice == CHOICE_RESTART) print ("you have decided to
restart");

if (userChoice == CHOICE_STOP) print ("you have decided to stop
the game");

if (userChoice == CHOICE_PAUSE) print ("you have decided to pause
the game");
```

In the previous code:

- We declare three **constant** variables.

- These variables are then used to check the choice made by the user.

In the next example, we use a constant to calculate a tax rate; this is a good practice as the same value will be used across the program with no or little room for errors when it comes to using the exact same tax rate across your program.

```
const float VAT_RATE = 0.21f;

float priceBeforeVat = 23.0f

float priceAfterVat = pricebeforeVat * VAT_RATE;
```

In the previous code:

- We declare a **constant** float variable for the vat rate.

- We declare a **float** variable for the item's price before tax.

- We calculate the item's price after adding the tax.

It is a very good coding practice to use constants for values that don't change across your program. Using constants makes your code more readable, it saves work when you need to change a value in your code, and it also decreases possible occurrences of errors (e.g., for calculations).

OPERATORS

Once we have declared and assigned values to variables, we can then combine these variables using operators. There are different types of operators including: arithmetic operators, assignment operators, comparison operators and logical operators. So let's look at each of these operators:

- **Arithmetic operators** are used to perform arithmetic operations including additions, subtractions, multiplications, or divisions. Common arithmetic operators include +, -, *, /, or % (modulo).

```
int number1 = 1;// the variable number1 is declared

int number2 = 1;// the variable number2 is declared

int sum = number1 + number2;// We add two numbers and store them
in the variable sum

int sub = number1 - number2;// We subtract two numbers and store
them in the variable sub
```

- **Assignment operators** can be used to assign a value to a variable and include =, +=, -=, *=, /= or %=.

```
int number1 = 1;

int number2 = 1;

number1+=1; //same as number1 = number1 + 1;

number1-=1; //same as number1 = number1 - 1;

number1*=1; //same as number1 = number1 * 1;

number1/=1; //same as number1 = number1 / 1;

number1%=1; //same as number1 = number1 % 1;
```

Note that the = operator, when used with strings, will concatenate these strings (i.e., add them one after the other to create a new string). When used with a number and a string, the same will apply; for example **"Hello"+1** will result in "**Hello1**".

- **Comparison operators** are often used in conditional statements to compare two values; comparison operators include ==, !=, >, <, <= and >=.

```
if (number1 == number2); //if number1 equals number2

if (number1 != number2); //if number1 and number2 have different
values

if (number1 > number2); //if number1 is greater than number2

if (number1 >= number2); //if number1 is greater than or equal to
number2

if (number1 < number2); //if number1 is less than number2

if (number1 <= number2); //if number1 is less than or equal to
number2
```

CONDITIONAL STATEMENTS

Statements can be performed based on a condition, and in this case, they are called **conditional statements**. The syntax is usually as follows:

```
if (condition) statement;
```

This means **if the condition is verified (or true) then (and only then) the statement is executed**. When we assess a condition, we test whether a declaration is true. For example, by typing **if (a == b)**, we mean **"if it is true that a is equal to b"**. Similarly, if we type **if (a>=b)** we mean **"if it is true that a is greater than or equal to b"**

As we will see later, we can also combine conditions and decide to perform a statement if two (or more) conditions are true. For example, by typing **if (a == b && c == 2)** we mean **"if a is equal to b and c is equal to 2"**. In this case, using the operator **&&** means **AND**, and that both conditions will need to be true. We could compare this to making a decision on whether we will go sailing tomorrow. For example, **"if the weather is sunny and if the wind speed is less than 5km/h then I will go sailing"**.

We could translate this statement as follows.

```
if (weatherIsSunny == true && windSpeed < 5) IGoSailing = true;
```

When creating conditions, as for most natural languages, we can use the operator **OR** noted **||**. Taking the previous example, we could translate the following sentence **"if the weather is too hot or if the wind is faster than 5km/h then I will not go sailing "**, as follows.

```
if (weatherIsTooHot == true || windSpeed >5) IGoSailing = false;
```

Another example could be as follows.

```
if (myName == "Patrick") print("Hello Patrick");
else print ("Hello Stranger");
```

In the previous code:

- We assess the value of the variable called **myName**.

- The statement **print("Hello Patrick")** will be printed if the value of the variable **myName** is **"Patrick"**.

- Otherwise, the message **"Hello Stranger"** will be displayed instead.

When we deal with combining true or false statements, we are effectively applying what is called **Boolean logic**. Boolean logic deals with Boolean variables that have two possible values 1 and 0 (or true and false). By evaluating conditions, we are effectively processing Boolean numbers and applying Boolean logic. While you don't need to know about Boolean logic in depth, some operators for Boolean logic are important, including the **!** operator. It means **NOT** (or "the opposite"). This means that if a variable is true, its opposite will be false, and vice versa. For example, if we consider the variable **weatherIsGood = true**, the value of **!weatherIsGood** will be **false** (its opposite). So the condition **if (weatherIdGood == false)** could be also written **if (!weatherIsGood)** which would literally translate as "if the weather is **NOT** good".

SWITCH STATEMENTS

If you have understood the concept of conditional statements, then this section should be pretty much straight forward. Switch statements are a variation on the if/else statements that we have seen earlier. The idea behind the switch statements is that, depending on the value of a particular variable, we will switch to a particular portion of the code and perform one or several actions accordingly. The variable considered for the switch structure is usually of type **integer**. Let's look at a simple example:

```
int choice = 1;
switch (choice)
{
    case 1:
        print ("you chose 1");
        break;
    case 2:
        print ("you chose 2");
        break;
    case 3:
        print ("you chose 3");
        break;
    default:
        print ("Default option");
        break;
}
print ("We have exited the switch structure");
```

In the previous code:

- We declare the variable called **choice**, as an **integer** and initialize it to **1**.

- We then create a **switch** structure whereby, depending on the value of the variable **choice**, the program will switch to the relevant section (i.e., the portion of code starting with **case 1:**, **case 2:**, etc.). Note that in our code, we look for the values **1**, **2** or **3**. However, if the variable **choice** is not equal to 1 or 2 or 3, the program will go to the section called **default**. This is because this section is executed if all of the other possible choices (i.e., 1, 2, or 3) have not been fulfilled (or selected).

Note that each choice or branch starts with the keyword **case** and ends with the keyword **break**. The **break** keyword is there to specify that after executing the commands included in the branch (or the current choice), the program should exit the switch structure. Without any break statement we will remain in the switch structure and the next line of code will be executed.

So let's consider the previous example and see how this would work in practice. In our case, the variable **choice** is set to **1**, so we will enter the **switch** structure, and then look for the section that deals with a value of **1** for the variable **choice**. This will be the section that starts with **case 1:**; then the command **print ("you chose 1");** will be executed, followed by the command **break**, indicating that we should exit the switch structure; finally the command **print ("We have exited the switch structure")** will be executed.

Switch structures are very useful to structure your code and when dealing with mutually exclusive choices (i.e., only one of the choices can be processed) based on an integer value, especially in the case of menus. In addition, switch structures make for cleaner and easily understandable code.

LOOPS

There are times when you have to perform repetitive tasks as a programmer; many times, these can be fast forwarded using loops which are structures that will perform the same actions repetitively based on a condition. So, the process is usually as follows when using loops:

- Start the loop.

- Perform actions.

- Check for a condition.

- Exit the loop if the condition is fulfilled or keep looping otherwise.

Sometimes the condition is performed at the start of the loop, some other times it is performed at the end of the loop. As we will see in the next paragraph this will be the case for the **while** and **do-while** loop structures, respectively.

Let's look at the following example that is using a **while** loop.

```
int counter =0;
while (counter <=10)
{
    counter++;
}
```

In the previous code:

- We declare the variable counter and set its value to 0.

- We then create a loop that starts with the keyword **while** and for which the content (which is what is to be executed while we are looping) is delimited by opening and closing curly brackets.

- We set the condition to remain in this loop (i.e., **counter <=10**). So we will remain in this loop as long as the variable counter is less than or equal to 10.

- Within the loop, we increase the value of the variable **counter** by 1 and print its value.

So effectively:

- The first time we go through the loop: the variable **counter** is increased to **1**; we reach the end of the loop; we go back to the start of the loop and check if **counter** is less or equal to **10**; this is true in this case because **counter** equals 1.

- The second time we go through the loop: **counter** is increased to **2**; we reach the end of the loop; we go back to the start of the loop and check if **counter** is less or equal to 10; this is true in this case because **counter** equals **2**.

- ...

- The 11th time we go through the loop: **counter** is increased to **11**; we reach the end of the loop; we go back to the start of the loop and check if **counter** is less or equal to 10; this is now false as **counter** now equals **11**. As a result, we exit the loop.

So, as you can see, using a loop, we have managed to increment the value of the variable **counter** iteratively, from 0 to 11, but using less code than would be needed otherwise.

Now, we could create a slightly modified version of this loop, using a **do-while** loop structure instead, as illustrated in the next example:

```
int counter =0;
do
{
    counter++;
} while (counter <=10);
```

In the previous example, you may spot two differences, compared to the previous code:

- The **while** keyword is now at the end of the loop. So the condition will be evaluated (or assessed) at the end of the loop.

- A **do** keyword is now featured at the start of the loop.

- So here, we perform statements first and then check for the condition at the end of the loop.

Another variations of the code could be as follows:

```
for (int counter = 0; counter <=10; counter ++)
{
        print ("Counter = " + counter);
}
```

In the previous code:

- We declare a loop in a slightly different way: we state that we will use an integer variable called **counter** that will go from 0 to 10.

- This variable **counter** will be incremented by 1 every time we go through the loop.

- We remain in the loop as long as the variable **counter** is less than or equal to 10.

- The test for the condition, in this case, is performed at the start of the loop.

Loops are very useful to be able to perform repetitive actions for a finite number of objects, or to perform what is usually referred as recursive actions. For example, you could use loops to create (or instantiate) 100 objects at different locations in your game, or to go through an array of 100 items. So using loops will definitely save you some code and time :-).

CLASSES

When coding in C# with Unity, you will be creating scripts that are either classes or that use built-in classes. So what is a class?

As we have seen earlier, C# is an object-oriented programming (OOP) language. Put simply, a C# program will consist of a collection of objects that interact with each other.

Each object has one or more attributes, and it is possible to perform actions on these objects using what are called **methods**. In addition, objects that share the same properties are said to belong to the same **class**. For example, we could take the analogy of a bike.

There are bikes of all shapes and colors; however, they share common features. For example, they all have a specific number of wheels (e.g., one, two or three wheels) or a speed; they can have a color, and actions can be performed on these bikes (e.g., accelerate, turn right, or turn left).

So in object-oriented programming, the class would the **Bike**, the speed or the color would be referred as **member variables**, and any action performed on the bike (i.e., accelerating) would be referred as a **member method**. So if we were to define a common type for all bikes, we could define a class called **Bike** and for this class define several member variables and attributes that would make it possible to define and perform actions on the objects of type **Bike**.

This is, obviously, a simplified explanation of classes and objects, but it should give you a clearer idea of the concept of object-oriented programming, if you are new to it.

DEFINING A CLASS

So now that you have a clearer idea of what a class is, let's see how we could define a class. So let's look at the following example.

```
public class Bike
{

    private float speed;

    private int color;


    private void accelerate()

    {

        speed++;

    }

    private void turnRight()

    {

    }

}
```

In the previous code, we have defined a class, called **Bike**, that includes two member variables (**speed** and **color**) as well as two member methods (**accelerate** and **turnRight**).

Let's look at the script a little closer and you may notice a few things:

- The name of the class is preceded by the keywords **public class**; in OOP terms, the keyword **public** is called an **access modifier** and it defines how (and from where) this class may be accessed and used. In C# there are at several types of access modifiers, including **public** (no restricted access), **protected** (access limited to the containing class or types derived from this class), **internal** (access is limited to the current assembly), or **private** (access only from the containing type).

- The names of all variables are preceded by their type (i.e., int), and the keyword **private**: this means that these variables will be accessible only for objects of types **Bike**.

- The name of each method is preceded by the keywords **private void**: the **void** keyword means that the method does not return any data back, while the keyword

private means that the method will be accessible only from the containing type (i.e., **Bike**). In other word, only objects of type **Bike** will be able to access this method.

ACCESSING CLASS MEMBERS AND VARIABLES

Once a class has been defined, it is great to be able to access its member variables and methods. In C#, and as for many other object-oriented programming languages, this can be done using the **dot notation**.

The dot notation refers to **object-oriented programming**. Using dots, you can access properties and functions (or methods) related to a particular object. For example **gameObject.transform.position** gives you access to the **position** from the **transform** of the object linked to this script. It is often useful to read it backward; in this case, the dot can be interpreted as **"of"**. So in our case, **gameObject.transform.position** can be translated as "the position **of** the transform **of** the **gameObject**".

Once a class has been defined, objects based on this class can be created. For example, if we were to create a new **Bike** object based on the code that we have seen above (i.e., based on the definition of the class **Bike**), the following code could be used.

```
Bike myBike = new Bike();
```

This code will create an object based on the "template" **Bike**. You may notice the syntax:

```
dataType variable = new dataType()
```

By default, this new object will include all the member variables and methods defined earlier. So it will have a color and a speed, and we should also be able to access its **accelerate** and **turnRight** methods. So how can this be done? Let's look at the next code snippet that shows how we can access member variables and methods.

```
Bike myBike = new Bike();
b.speed = 12.3f
b.color = 2;
b.accelerate();
```

In the previous code:

- The new bike **myBike** is created.

- Its speed is set to **12.3** and its color is set to **2**.

- The speed is then increased after calling the **accelerate** method.

- Note that to assign an object's attribute or method, we use the dot notation.

When defining member variables and methods, it is usually good practice to restrict the access to member variables (e.g., private type) and to define public methods with no or less strict restrictions (e.g., public) that provide access to these variables. These methods are often referred to as **getters** and **setters**, because you can **get** or **set** member values through these methods.

To illustrate this concept, let's look at the following code:

```
public class Bike
{
    private float speed;
    private int color;


    private void accelerate()
    {
        speed++;
    }
    public void setSpeed (float newSpeed)
    {
        speed = newSpeed;
    }
    public float getSpeed ()
    {
        return (speed)
    }
    private void turnRight()
    {
    }
}
```

In the previous code, we have declared two new methods: **setSpeed** and **getSpeed**.

- For **setSpeed**: the type is **void** as this method does not return any information, and its access is set to **public**, so that it can be employed with no restrictions.

- For **getSpeed**: the return type is **float** as this method returns the speed, which type is float. Its access is set to **public**, so that it can be accessed with no restrictions.

So, we could combine the code that we have created so far in one program (or a new class) as follows in Unity.

```csharp
using UnityEngine;
using System.Collections;
public class TestCode : MonoBehaviour {
    public class Bike
    {
        private float speed;
        private int color;
        private void accelerate(){speed++;}
        public void setSpeed (float newSpeed)
        {
            speed = newSpeed;
        }
        public float getSpeed (){return (speed);}
        private void turnRight(){}
    }
    public void Start ()
    {
        Bike myBike = new Bike();
        myBike.setSpeed (23.0f);
        print (myBike.getSpeed());
    }
}
```

In this code, you may notice at least two differences compared to the previous code snippet:

- At the start of the code, the following two lines of code have been added:

```
using UnityEngine;

using System.Collections;
```

- The keyword **using** is called a directive; in this particular context it is used to import what is called a **namespace**; put simply, by adding this directive you are effectively gaining access to a collection of classes or data types. Each of these namespaces or "libraries" includes useful classes for your program. For example, the namespace **UnityEngine** will include classes for Unity development and **System.Collections** will include classes and interfaces for different collections of objects. By default, whenever you create a new C# script in Unity, these two namespaces (and associated directives) are included.

- We have declared our class **Bike** within another class called **TestCode** that is, in this case, the containing class.

```
public class TestCode : MonoBehaviour {
```

- Whenever you create a new C# script, the name of the script (for example **TestCode** will be used to define the main class within the script (i.e., **TestCode**).

- The syntax "**: Monobehavior**" means that the class **TestCode** is derived from the class **MonoBehaviour**. This is often referred to as **inheritance**.

CONSTRUCTORS

As we have seen in the previous sections, when a new object is created, it will, by default, include all the member variables and methods of its class. To create this object, we would typically use the name of the class followed by an opening and closing round bracket as per the next example.

```
Bike myBike = new Bike();
myBike.color = 2;
myBike.speed = 12.3f;
```

In fact, it is possible to change some of the properties of the newly created object when it is initialized. For example, instead of setting the speed and the color of the object, as we have done in the previous code, it would be great to be able to set these automatically and to pass the parameters accordingly when the object is created. This can be done with what is called a **constructor**. A constructor literally helps to construct your new object based on parameters (also referred as arguments) and instructions. So, for example, let's say that we would like the color of our bike to be specified when it is created; we could modify the **Bike** class, as follows, by adding the following method:

```
public Bike (int newColor)
{
        color = newColor;
}
```

This is a new constructor (the name of the method is the same as the class), and it takes an integer as a parameter; so after modifying the description of our class (as per the previous code), we could then create a new **Bike** object as follows:

```
Bike myBike = new Bike(2);
//myBike.color = 2;
myBike.speed = 12.3f;
```

We could even specify a second constructor that would include both the color and the speed as follows:

```
public Bike (int newColor, float newSpeed)
{
    color = newColor;
    speed = newSpeed;
}
```

You can have different constructors in your class; the constructor used at the instantiation stage (i.e., when a new object is created based on an existing class) will be the one that matches the arguments that have been passed.

For example, let's say that we have two constructors for our **Bike** class, as follows:

```
public Bike (int newColor, float newSpeed)
{
    color = newColor;
    speed = newSpeed;
}
public Bike (int newColor)
{
    color = newColor;
}
```

If a new **Bike** object is created as follows:

```
Bike newBike = new Bike (2)
```

…then the first constructor will be called.

If a new **Bike** object is created as follows:

```
Bike newBike = new Bike (2, 10.0f)
```

…then the second constructor will be called.

You may also wonder what happens if the following code is used, since no default constructor has been defined.

```
Bike newBike = new Bike ();
```

In fact, whenever you create your class, a default constructor is also defined implicitly and evoked whenever a new object is created using the **new** operator with no arguments. This is called a default constructor. In this case, the default values for each of the types of the numerical member variables are used (e.g., 0 is the default value for integers and false is the default value for Boolean variables).

Note that access to constructors is usually public, except in the particular cases where we would like a class not to be instantiated (e.g., for classes that include **static** members only). Also note that, as for variables, if no access modifiers are specified, member variables will be **private** by default. This is similar for methods.

DESTRUCTORS

As for constructors, when an object is deleted, the corresponding destructor is called. Its name is the same as the class and it is preceded by a tilde ~; as illustrated in the next code snippet.

```
~Bike()//this is the destructor
{
        print("Object has been destroyed");
}
```

This being said, a destructor can neither take parameters (or arguments) nor return a value.

STATIC MEMBER VARIABLES AND METHODS

When a method or a variable is declared as **static**, only one instance of this member exists for a class. So a static variable will be "shared" between instances of this class.

Static variables are usually employed to retrieve constants without instantiating a class. The same applies for static method: they can be evoked without the need to instantiate a class.

This can be very useful if you want to create and avail of tools to manipulate data or objects without the need for instantiation. For example, in Unity, it is possible to use the method **GameObject.Find**(); this method usually makes it possible to look for a particular object based on its name. Let's look at the following example.

```
public void  Start()
{
    GameObject t = (GameObject) GameObject.Find("test");
}
```

In the previous code, we look for an object called **test**, and we store the result inside the variable **t** of type **GameObject**. However, when we use the syntax **GameObject.Find**, we use the static method **Find** that is available from the class **GameObject**. There are many other static functions that you will be able to use in Unity, including **Instantiate**. Again, these functions can be called without the need to instantiate an object. The following code snippet provides another example based on the class **Bike**. The following code illustrates the use of static variables.

```csharp
using UnityEngine;
using System.Collections;

public class TestCode : MonoBehaviour {

    public class Bike
    {
        private float speed;
        private int color;
        private static nbBikes;
        private int countBikes()
        {
            nbBikes++;
        }
        private int getNbBikes()
        {
            return(nbBikes);
        }
    }
    public void Start ()
    {
        Bike bike1 = new Bike();
        Bike bike2 = new Bike();
        bike1.countBikes();
        bike2.countBikes();
        print("Nb Bikes:"+getNbBikes());

    }
}
```

In the previous code:

The member variable **nbBikes** is static and will be shared between all instanced of the class Bike.

- We create a method called **countBikes** that will increase the value of the variable **nbBikes** every time it is called.

- We then instantiate two bikes, **bike1** and **bike2**.

- We also call the method **countBikes** from both bikes (i.e., from **bike1** and **bike2**).

- Finally, we print the value of the variable **nbBikes**.

- This code should display the message "**NB bikes 2**".

The following code illustrates the use of static functions.

```
using UnityEngine;
using System.Collections;


public class TestCode : MonoBehaviour {


    public class Bike
    {
        private float speed; private int color;
        public static sayHello(){print ("Hello");}
    }
    public void Start (){Bike.sayHello();}
}
```

The previous code would result in the following output:

```
Hello
```

In the previous code, we declare a static method called **sayHello**; this method is then called from the **Start** method without the need to instantiate (or create) a new **Bike**. This is because, due to its **public** and **static** attributes, the method **sayHello** can be accessed from anywhere in the program.

INHERITANCE

I hope everything is clear so far, as we are going to look at a very interesting and important principle for object-oriented programming: **inheritance**. The main idea behind inheritance is that objects can inherit their properties from other objects (i.e., their parents). As they inherit these properties, the new objects (i.e., the children) can be identical to the parents or evolve and overwrite some of their inherited properties. This is very interesting because it makes it possible to minimize your code by creating a class with general properties for all objects that share similar features, and then, if need be, to overwrite and customize some of these properties.

Let's take the example of vehicles; generally, vehicles have some of the following properties:

- Number of wheels.

- Speed.

- Number of passengers.

- Color.

- Capacity to accelerate.

- Capacity to stop.

So we could create the following class for example:

```
class Vehicles
{

    private int nbWheels;

    private float speed;

    private int nbPassengers;

    private int color;

    private void accelerate()
    {

        speed++;

    }

}
```

In the previous code, we have defined a class called **Vehicles** that includes four member variables and a member method called **accelerate**.

The member variables defined in this class (i.e., **nbWheels**, speed, **nbPasssengers**, or **color**) could apply to cars, bikes, motorbikes, or trucks. However, all these vehicles also differ; some of them may or may not have an engine or a steering wheel, for example. So we could create a subclass called **MotorizedVehicles**, based on the class **Vehicles**, but with specificities linked to the fact that they are motorized. These added attributes could be as follows:

- Engine size.

- Petrol type.

- Petrol levels.

- Ability to fill-up the tank.

The following example illustrates how this class could be created.

```
class MotorizedVehicles: Vehicles
{
     private float engineSize;

     private int petrolType;

     private float petrolLevels;

     private void fillUpTank()
     {
          petrolLevels+=10;
     }
}
```

In the previous code:

- We create a new class called **MotorizedVehicles** that inherits from the class **Vehicles**.

- When the class is defined, its name is followed by "**: Vehicles**". This means that it inherits from the class **Vehicles**. So it will, by default, avail of all the methods and variables already included in the class **Vehicles**.

- We have created a new member method for this class, called **fillUpTank**.

- In the previous example, you may notice that the methods and variables that were defined for the class **Vehicles** do not appear in the code snippet; this is because they are implicitly added to this new class, since it inherits from the class **Vehicles**.

Whenever you create a new class in Unity, it will, by default, inherit from the **MonoBehaviour** class; as a result, it will implicitly include all the member methods and variables of the class **MonoBehaviour**. Some of these methods include **Start** or **Update**, for example.

When using inheritance, the parent is usually referred to as the **base class**, while the child is referred to as the **inherited class**.

Now, while the child inherits **behaviors** and **attributes** from its parents, these can always be modified or, put simply, overwritten. However, in this case, the base method (the method defined in the parent) must be declared as virtual. Also, when overriding this method, the keyword **override** must be used. This is illustrated in the following code.

```
class Vehicles
{

    private int nbWheels;

    private float speed;

    private int nbPassengers;

    private int color;

    private virtual void accelerate()
    {

        speed++;

    }
}
class MotoredVehicles: Vehicles
{

    private float engineSize;

    private int petrolType;

    private float petrolLevels;

    private void fillUpTank()
    {

        petrolLevels+=10;

    }
    private override void accelerate()
    {

        speed+=10;

    }
}
```

In the previous example, while the method **accelerate** is inherited from the class **Vehicles**, it would normally increase the speed by one. However, by overwriting it, we make sure that in the case of objects instantiated from the class **MotoredVehicles**, each acceleration increases the speed by **10** instead.

There are obviously more concepts linked to inheritance; however, the information provided in this section should get you started easily. For more information on inheritance in C#, you can <u>look at the official documentation</u>.

METHODS

Methods or functions can be compared to a friend or colleague to whom you gently ask to perform a task, based on specific instructions, and to return the information to you then, if need be. For example, you could ask your friend the following: "**Can you please tell me when I will be celebrating my 20th birthday given that I was born in 2000**". So you give your friend (who is good at Math :-)) the information (i.e., date of birth) and s/he will calculate the year of your 20th birthday and then give you this information. So in other words, your friend will be given an input (for example, the date of birth) and return an output (for example, the year of your 20th birthday).

Methods work exactly this way: they are given information (and sometimes not), they perform an action, and then, if needed, they return information.

In programming terms, a method (or a function) is a block of instructions that performs a set of actions. It is executed when invoked (or put more simply, when it is **called**) from the script, or when an event occurs (for example, when the player has clicked on a button or when the player collides with an object). Member methods need to be declared before they can be called.

Methods are very useful because once the code for a method has been created, this method can be called several times without the need to re-write the same code over and over again. Also, because a method can take parameters, it can process these parameters and produce (or return) information accordingly; in other words, a method can perform different actions and produce different results depending on the input. So methods can do one or all of the following:

- Take parameters and process them.

- Perform an action.

- Return a result.

A method has a syntax and can be declared as in at least two ways.

```
AccessType typeOfDataReturned nameOfTheFunction ()
{
        Perform actions here...
}
```

In the previous code the method does not take any input; neither does it return an output. It just performs actions.

OR

```
AccessType typeOfDataReturned nameOfTheFunction
(typeOfParameater1 param1, typeOfParameater2 param2)
{
    Perform actions here...
}
```

Let's look at the following method for example.

```
public int calculateSum(int a, int b)
{
    return (a+b);
}
```

In the previous code:

- The method is of access type **public** and it can be accessed without restriction.

- The method will return an integer.

- The name of the method is **calculateSum**.

- The method takes two integer arguments (or parameters).

- The method returns the sum of the two parameters that were passed to this function. These parameters will be referred as **a** and **b** within this method.

A method can be called using its name followed by an opening and closing round bracket, as follows:

```
nameOfTheFunction1();
nameOfTheFunction2(value);
int test = nameOfTheFunction3(value);
```

In the previous code:

- A method is called with no parameter (line 1).

- A method is called with a parameter (line 2).

- In the third example (line 3), a variable called **test** will be set with the value returned by the method **nameOfTheFunction3**.

You may, and we will get to this later, have different methods in a class with the exact same name but each of these methods may require a different number and different types of parameters. This is often referred as polymorphism, as the method literally takes different forms and can process information differently based on the information (e.g., type of data) provided.

ACCESSING METHODS AND ACCESS MODIFIERS

As we have seen previously, in C# there are different types of access modifiers. These modifiers specify from where a method can be called. Common modifiers include:

- **public**: this means that there is no restricted access.

- **protected**: this means that access is limited to the containing class or types derived from this class.

- **internal**: this means that access is limited to the current assembly.

- **private**: this means that access is limited to the containing type.

OVERLOADING

Overloading is a concept linked to polymorphism, whereby a method can take different forms. By overloading a method, you can create multiple methods with the same name but with a different number and types of parameters. Let's look at the following example:

```
public class MyBike
{
    int speed;
    void accelerate()
    {
        speed++;
    }
    void accelerate (int increment)
    {
        speed = speed+ increment;
    }
    void runBike()
    {
        accelerate();
        accelerate(10);
    }
}
```

In the previous code:

- We declare a new class called **MyBike**.

- We also declare a member variable called **speed**.

- We then create two methods named **accelerate**.

- The first method takes no parameters and it will increase the speed of the bike by one every time it is called.

- The second method will also increase the speed of the bike; however, it takes a parameter that will be used to specify by how much the speed should be increased.

- Then the method **runBike** is declared; it calls the two methods **accelerate**;

- The code **accelerate();** calls the first **accelerate** method. This is because no parameter is passed to the method accelerate, so it is assumed that we refer to the first version of the **accelerate** method.

- The code **accelerate(10);** calls the second **accelerate** method. This is because an integer parameter is passed to the method this time, so it is assumed that we refer to the second **accelerate** method.

So in other words, you can overload functions by creating multiple functions with the same name as long as their argument list (i.e., the number and the types of the arguments) is different.

LOCAL, MEMBER AND GLOBAL VARIABLES

Whenever you create a variable in C#, you will need to be aware of the scope and access type of this variable so that you know where it can be used.

The scope of a variable refers to where you can use this variable in a script. In C#, we usually make the difference between **member variables** and **local variables**.

You can compare the term **local** and **member** variables to a language that is either local or global. In the first case, the local language will only be used (i.e., spoken) by the locals, whereas the global language will be used (i.e., spoken) and understood by anyone whether they are locals or part of the global community.

When you create a class definition along with member variables, these variables will be seen by any method within your class.

Member variables are variables that can be used anywhere in your class, hence the name **member**. These variables need to be declared at the start of the script (using the usual declaration syntax) and outside of any method; they can then be used anywhere in the class as illustrated in the next code snippet.

```
class MyBike
{
    private int color;
    private float speed;


    public void accelerate()
    {
        speed++;
    }
}
```

In the previous code, for example, we declare the variable **speed** as a member variable and we access it from the method accelerate.

Local variables are declared within a method and are to be used only within this method, hence the term local, because they can only be used locally, as illustrated in the next code snippet.

```
public void  Start()
{
     int myVar;

     myVar = 0;
}
public void Update()
{
     int myVar2;

     myVar2 = 2;
}
```

In the previous code, **myVar** is a local variable to the method **Start**, and can only be used within this function; **myVar2** is a local variable to the method **Update**, and can only be used within this method.

Last but not least, you can create member variables that can be accessed from anywhere in your game. To do so, this variable will need to be declared as a **public static member variable** as follows:

```
class MyBike
{
     public static nbBikes;
     private int color;
     private float speed;


     public void accelerate()
     {
          speed++;
     }
}
```

The reason for the global variable **nbBikes** to be accessible throughout your game is because it is both public (i.e., accessible from anywhere) and static (i.e., shared across your game).

POLYMORPHISM (GENERAL CONCEPTS)

The word polymorphism takes its meaning from **poly** (several) and **morph** (shape); so it literally means several forms. In object-oriented programming, it refers to the ability to process objects differently depending on their data type or class. Let's take the example of a simple addition. If we want to add two numbers, we just make an algebraic addition (for example, 1 + 2). However, adding two **string** variables may mean concatenating them, which means adding them one after the other. For example, adding the text "**Hello**" and the text "**World**" would result in the text "**HelloWorld**". As you can see, the result of an operation may depend on the data types involved. So again, with polymorphism we will be able to customize methods (or operations) so that data is processed based on its type of class. So, let's look at the following code which illustrates how this can be done in C#.

```
public class AddObjects
{
    public int add (int a, int b)
    {
        return (a + b);
    }
    public string add (string a, string b)
    {
        return (a + b);
    }
}
```

In the previous code, it is possible to add two different types of data: integers and strings. Depending on whether two integers or two strings are passed as parameters, we will be calling either the first **add** method or the second **add** method.

The decision on whether the first or second version of the method **add** is called will be made at compilation time, because we know, before the script is compiled, what method should be called depending on the number of types of the variables passed to this method; this is, therefore, called **static polymorphism**. The term static means that after compiling our script we still know for sure that a particular piece of code will call a specific function; for example, in our case, if we add the code **add (2 , 2)** to our script before compilation, we know for sure that after compilation the first version of the function add will be called.

DYNAMIC POLYMORPHISM AND OVERRIDING

As we have seen in the previous section, static polymorphism can be achieved by using, for example, overloaded methods. This being said, there are times when we won't effectively know what code will be executed when we call a function at run-time, and this can be, for example, seen in (and implemented through) dynamic polymorphism.

In dynamic polymorphism, although we may know the name of the method to be called, the actual actions performed by the functions may vary at run-time (hence the term **dynamic**).

In C#, dynamic polymorphism can be achieved using both abstract classes and virtual functions.

In C#, it is possible to create a class that will provide a partial implementation of an interface. Broadly, an interface defines what a class should include (for example, the member methods, the member variables or some events), but it does not declare how these should be implemented. So, an abstract class will include abstract methods or variables. This means that this class will define the name and the type of the member variables, the name and the types of parameters for member methods, as well as the type of data returned by these methods. This type of class is called **abstract** because such classes cannot be instantiated. However, these classes can be used as a template (or "dream" class) for derived classes. Let's look at the following example to illustrate this concept.

```
abstract class Vehicule
{
    public abstract void decelerate();
}


class Bike: Vehicule
{
    private float speed;
    private int color;
    public Bike (float newSpeed)
    {
        speed = newSpeed;
    }
    public override void decelerate()
    {
        speed --;
    }
}
```

In the previous code:

- We declare an abstract class **Vehicle**.

- We declare an abstract method called **decelerate**.

- We then create a new class called **Bike**, inherited from the abstract class **Vehicle**.

- We then override the abstract method **decelerate** to use our own implementation.

Using an abstract class just means that we list methods that would be useful for the children; however, the children classes will have to define how the method should be implemented.

The second way to implement dynamic polymorphism is by using **virtual** methods or variables. In the case of **virtual methods**, we declare a method that will be used by default by objects of this class or inherited classes; however, in this case, even if the method is ready to be used (this is because we have defined how it should be implemented), it can be changed (or overridden) by the child (or the inherited class) to fit a specific purpose. In this case (i.e., inherited method), we need to specify that we **override** the method that was initially implemented by the parent by using the keyword **override**.

The key difference between an abstract and a virtual method is that, while an abstract method should be overridden, a virtual method may be overridden if the base method (which is the method declared in the base or parent class) does not suit a particular purpose.

Let's look at the following example to illustrate the concept of virtual methods:

```csharp
class Vehicule
{

    private float speed;
    public virtual accelerate()
    {
        speed +=10;
    }
}


class Bike: Vehicule
{

    public override accelerate()
    {
        speed++;
    }
}
```

In the previous code:

- We declare a class **Vehicle**.

- It includes both a private variable **speed** and a virtual method called **accelerate**. This method is virtual, which means the child classes (which are the classes inheriting from the class **Vehicle**) will be able to modify (or **override**) it, if need be.

[73]

- We then create a new class **Bike** that inherits form the class **Vehicle**. In this class, we override the method **accelerate** using the keyword **override** so that the speed is just incremented by one.

NameSpaces

When you create a new script in Unity, it usually includes the following lines at the top of the script automatically.

```
using System.Collections;

using System.Collections.Generic;

using UnityEngine;
```

This code is effectively specifying the location of some classes that you may use in your code, and provides information about what namespace (which is comparable to a folder or directory) a specific class belongs to. This is to avoid any clash or confusion and to ensure that even if a class is declared in two different namespaces, that it is clear as to which class (and namespace) you want to use.

So what is a name space?

Namespaces are containers within which you can declare classes; let's look at the following example:

```csharp
namespace NameSpace1
{
    public class MyClass
    {
        public static int add(int a, int b)
        {
            return (a + b);
        }
    }
}


namespace NameSpace2
{
    public class MyClass
    {
        public static int add(int a, int b, int c)
        {
            return (a + b + c);
        }
    }
}
```

In the previous code:

- We declare two namespaces called **NameSpace1** and **NameSpace2**.

- Within these namespaces, that act as containers, we declare a class called **MyClass**.

- So we have two classes with the exact same name (i.e., **MyClass**); however, we can manage to tell them apart based on their namespace (or their container).

Now that the two different namespaces have been defined, we need to find a way to specify which namespace will be used when classes with the same name are used or instantiated.

This can be done in at least two ways. The first way is to implicitly mention the namespace and the nested class within. For example, we could write the following code to refer to the first class, as illustrated in the next code snippet.

```
using System.Collections;
using System.Collections.Generic;
using UnityEngine;


public class MyNAmeSpacesExample : MonoBehaviour
{
    void Start ()
    {
        int sum1 = NameSpace1.MyClass.add(1,2);
        int sum2 = NameSpace2.MyClass.add(1,2,3);
        print ("Sum1:" + sum1 + "; Sum2:" + sum2);
    }
}
```

In the previous code:

- We access the method **add,** that is both public and static, from the class **MyClass** that is within the namespace **NameSpace1**.

- We also access the method **add** (that is both public and static) from the class **MyClass** that is within the namespace **NameSpace2**.

- The **add** method that is used in the previous example is **public**, so it can be accessed from anywhere in our programme; it is also **static** so it can be accessed without the need to instantiate an object of the class **MyClass**.

Another way to do this is to specify, from the very start of the script, that we will be using the namespaces **NameSpace1** or **NameSpace2**, and this can be done with the keyword called **using** as follows:

```
using System.Collections;

using System.Collections.Generic;

using UnityEngine;

using NameSpace1;


public class MyNameSpacesExample : MonoBehaviour
{
    void Start ()
    {
        int sum1 = MyClass.add(1,2);
        print ("Sum1:" + sum1);
    }
}
```

In the previous code:

- We declare (or we make a reference to) the namespace **NameSpace1**.

- This means that, if in doubt about where to find a particular class, it may be found in this namespace.

- We then call the method **add**; however, because we have defined a reference to the namespace **NameSpace1**, the system will automatically look into this namespace to find the class **MyClass** and the method **add**.

So how can namespaces be used in Unity?

Using namespaces in Unity can make your code more concise and it can also save you a lot of time. For example, let's say that you want to write some text onscreen through UI objects (such as UI Text objects) from your script. In this case, you may use code that is similar to the following:

```
using System.Collections;

using System.Collections.Generic;

using UnityEngine;

using UnityEngine.UI;


public class NameSpaceForUI : MonoBehaviour

{


    // Use this for initialization
    void Start () {
        GameObject.Find ("TextUI").GetComponent<Text> ().text
= "";

        GameObject.Find ("scoreUI").GetComponent<Text> ().text
= "Score:";


    }

}
```

In the previous code, we declare that we will be using the **UI** namespace with the code:

```
using UnityEngine.UI;
```

If we had not used the namespace **UnityEngine.UI**, the following line

```
GameObject.Find ("TextUI").GetComponent<Text> ().text = "";
```

may have needed to be written as follows instead:

```
GameObject.Find ("TextUI").GetComponent<UnityEngine.UI.Text>
().text = "";
```

So by specifying the namespace **UnityEngine.UI** we can shorten our code and use **GetComponent<Text>** or **GetComponent<Slider>** as both the **Text** and **Slider** classes are part of the namespace **UnityEngine.UI**.

More often than not, you may not need to use additional namespaces in Unity unless you create your own library. However, as illustrated previously, it can be useful to shorten your code when classes from the same namespace are employed several times.

When creating your scripts, you may wonder when you need the following statements:

```
using System.Collections;
using System.Collections.Generic;
using UnityEngine;
```

Whether you will need to use these lines depends on what you need to perform in your code:

- The namespace **UnityEngine**: most of your scripts will be linked to **GameObjects**, and will therefore need to extend the class **MonoBehaviour**; since the class **MonoBehaviour** belongs to the **UnityEngine** namespace, you will, in most cases, need this line. In addition, several useful classes are provided within the UnityEngine namespace.

- The namespace **System.Collections**: this namespace includes many basic classes including **IEnumerators** which are often used for coroutines.

- The namespace **System.Collections.Generic**: this namespace includes some useful classes provided by C# including Lists or Dictionaries.

So, if you need to keep one of these, you may keep **UnityEngine**, although, it is good practice to keep all three lines, just in case they may be needed later in your class.

LISTS

As we have seen in the previous sections, it is sometimes useful to employ arrays. However, when you are dealing with a large amount of data, or data that is meant to grow overtime, lists may be more useful, as they include built-in tools to sort and organize your data.

In addition, lists are generally more efficient as your data grows. So, you don't always need to use lists; however, they may be more efficient to organize your data, especially for large and evolving data sets.

So let's look into **Lists**.

You can declare a list as follows:

```
List <int> myList;
```

The declaration follows the syntax:

```
List <type> nameOfVariable;
```

So you could create a list of integers, strings, or Cubes if you wished.

Once the list has been created, C# offers several built-in methods that make it possible to manipulate a list, including:

- **Add**: adds an item at the end of the list.
- **Insert**: inserts an item at a specific index.
- **Remove**: removes an item from the list.
- **RemoveAt**: removes an item at a specific index
- **Count**: returns the number of items in a list.
- **Sort**: sorts the elements of a list.

Each element in the list has a default index that is relative to when it was first added to the list; the earlier the item is added to the list and the lower the index. So the first item added to the list will have, by default, the index 0, the second item will have the index 1, and so on. Let's look at an example:

```
List <string> listOfNames = new List<string> ();
listOfNames.Add ("Mary");
listOfNames.Add ("Paul");
print ("Size of List" + listOfNames.Count);
//this will display "Size of list 2"
listOfNames.Remove("Paul");
print ("Size of List after removing" + listOfNames.Count);
//this will display "Size of list 1"
```

In the previous code:

- We create a new list of **string** variables.

- We then add two elements to the list: the strings **Mary** and **Paul**.

- We display the size of the list before and after an item has been removed from the list.

DICTIONARIES

Lists are very useful, and dictionaries, which are special type of lists, take this concept a step further. With dictionaries, you can define a dataset with different records, and each record is accessible through a key instead of an index; for example, let's consider a class of students, each with a first name, a last name, and a student number. To represent and manage this data, we could create code similar to the following:

```
public class Student{

    public string firstName;

    public string lastName;

    public Student(string fName, string lName)
    {
        firstName = fName;

        lastName = lName;

    }
}
```

- We could then create code that uses this class as follows:

```
Dictionary<string, Student> students = new Dictionary<string, Student>();

students.Add("ST123",new Student("Mary", "Black"));

students.Add("ST124",new Student("John", "Hennessy"));

print ("Name of student ST124 is " + students ["ST124"].firstName);
```

In the previous code:

- We declare a dictionary of **Students**.

- When declaring the dictionary: the first parameter, which is a **string**, is used as an **index** or a **key**; this index will be the **student id**.

- The second parameter will be an object of type **Student**.

- So effectively we create a link between the **key** and the **Student** object.

- We then add students to our dictionary.

- When using the **Add** method, the first parameter is the **key** (or the **student id** in our case: **ST123** or **ST124** here), and the second parameter is the student object. This student object is created by calling the constructor of the class **Student** and by passing relevant parameters to the constructor, such as the student's first name and last name.

- Finally, we print the **first name** of a specific student based on its **student id**.

As for lists, Dictionaries have several built-in functions that make it easier to manipulate them, including:

- **Add**: to add a new item to the dictionary.

- **ContainsKey**: to check if a record with a specific key exists in the dictionary.

- **Remove**: to remove an item from the dictionary.

EVENTS

Put simply, events can be compared to something that happens at a particular time. When this event occurs, something (an action for example) needs to be performed. To simplify things, we could draw an analogy between events and daily activities: when your alarm goes off in the morning (which is an event) you can either get-up (this is an action) or decide to go back to sleep. Similarly, when you receive an email (this is another event), you can decide to read it (this is another action), and then reply to the sender (another action).

In computer terms, the concept of **events** is relatively similar, although the events that we will be dealing with in C# will be slightly different to the ones we just mentioned. For example, we could be waiting for the user to press a key (an event) and then move the character accordingly (an action), or wait until the user clicks on a button on screen (an event) to load a new scene (which is an action).

Usually in Unity, whenever an event occurs, a function is called. The function, in this case, is often referred as a handler, because it "handles" the event that just occurred. You have then the opportunity to modify this function and to add instructions (which include statements) that should be executed when this event occurs.

> To draw an analogy with daily activities: we could write instructions to a friend on a piece of paper, so that, in case someone calls in our absence, this friend knows exactly what to do. So an event handler is basically a set of instructions, usually stored within a function, that need to be followed in case a particular event occurs.

Sometimes information is passed to this method about the particular event that just occurred, and sometimes not. For example, in Unity, when the screen is refreshed the method **Update** is called. When a particular script is enabled, the method **Start** is called. When there is a collision between the player and an object, the method **OnControllerColliderHit** is called. For this particular event (which is a collision), an object is usually passed to the method that handles the event so that we get to know more about the other object involved in the collision.

As you can see, many events can occur in our game, and in your games, you will more than likely be dealing with the following events:

- **Start**: when a script is enabled (e.g., start of the scene).

- **Update**: when the screen is refreshed (e.g., every frame).

- **OnControllerColliderHit**: when a collision occurs between the player and another object.

- **Awake**: when the game starts (i.e., once throughout the lifetime of your game).

LEVEL ROUNDUP

In this chapter, we have learned some concepts related to C# and Object-Oriented Programming. We also learnt how to define and to use classes, along with member variables and methods. Along the way, we also looked at other programming concepts such as variables, loops, and conditional statements. So, we have covered considerable ground to get you started with C#!

Checklist

You can consider moving to the next stage if you can do the following:

- Understand the concept of Object-Oriented Programming.

- Understand the meaning of classes, member variables and member methods.

- Understand the role of a constructor.

- Understand the role of access modifiers.

Quiz

Now, let's check your knowledge! Please answer the following questions or specify if these statements are either correct or incorrect (the solutions are on the next page).

1. The value of a variable always remains constant.

2. A method always returns information.

3. A method may not return information.

4. If a method is void, it will return an integer value.

5. An array can store several variables at a time.

6. A class usually includes a constructor.

7. A for loop can be used to go through all the elements of an array.

8. A public method is accessible from anywhere.

9. A private variable is accessible only from members of the class.

10. A protected variable is accessible only from members of the class.

Solutions to the Quiz

1. False.

2. False.

3. True.

4. False.

5. True.

6. True.

7. True.

8. True.

9. True.

10. False (also from the children).

2
CREATING YOUR FIRST SCRIPT

In this section we will start to create C# scripts in Unity. Some of the objectives of this section will be to:

- Introduce C# scripting in Unity.

- Explain some basic scripting concepts.

- Explain how to display information from the code to the **Console** window.

- Illustrate how to create classes and to employ object-oriented principles.

After completing this chapter, you will be able to:

- Understand and apply basic C# concepts.

- Understand best coding practices.

- Code your first script in Unity.

- Create classes, methods and variables.

- Instantiate objects based on your own classes.

- Use built-in methods.

- Use common structures such as conditional statements or loops.

You can skip this chapter if you are already familiar with C#, or if you have already created and used C# scripts within Unity.

WORKFLOW TO CREATE A SCRIPT

There are many ways to create and use scripts in Unity, but generally the process is as follows:

- Create a new script using the **Project** view (**Create | C# Script)**, the main menu (**Assets | Create | C# Script**) or from an object via the **Inspector** (using the option **Add Component**).

- Attach the script to an object (for example, drag and drop the script on the object).

- Check in the **Console** window that there are no errors in the script.

- Play the scene.

By default, when you create your script, the name of the class within the script will be the same name as your script. So let's say that you created a new script called **TestCode**, then the following code will be automatically generated.

```
using UnityEngine;
using System.Collections;


public class TestCode : MonoBehaviour
{

    public void Start ()
    {
    }
    public void Update ()
    {
    }
}
```

- In the previous code, the class **TestCode** has been created; it inherits from the class **MonoBehaviour** and it includes two methods that can be modified: the methods **Start** and **Update**.

- You will also notice the two namespaces **UnityEngine** and **System.Collections**. As we have seen earlier, the keywords **using** is called a directive; in this particular case it is used to specify the namespaces and classes that will be used in our script.

- If you would like to know more about namespaces and directives, you may look at the section called **NameSpaces** in the previous chapter.

HOW SCRIPTS ARE COMPILED

Whenever you create and save a script, it is compiled, and Unity will notify you (using the **Console** window) of any error. This being said, the order in which a script is compiled depends on its location.

First, the scripts located in the folders **Standard Assets**, **Pro Standard Assets or Plugins** are compiled, then the scripts located in the folders **Standard Assets/Editor**, **Pro Assets/Editor** or **Plugins/Editor** are compiled, then the scripts outside the **Editor** folder are compiled, followed by the scripts in the **Editor** folder. For more information on script compilation, you can check the official documentation.

CODING CONVENTIONS

Quite often, coding conventions can provide increased clarity for your code and can be applied depending on the language that is being used.

Naming conventions usually employ a combination of **Camel casing** and **Pascal casing**.

- In **Camel casing** all words included in a name, except for the first one, are capitalized (e.g., my<u>V</u>ariable).

- In **Pascal casing** all words included in a name are capitalized (e.g., MyVariable).

When coding in C#, for example, naming conventions will use a combination of Camel and Pascal casing depending on whether you are naming a class, an interface, a variable or a resource.

However, as a C# beginner, in addition to learning about classes, methods, or inheritance, it may not be necessary to completely adhere to this naming convention at the start, at least as long as you use a consistent naming scheme throughout your code.

So, it is good to acknowledge different naming conventions linked to programming languages and to understand why they are in place; however, to keep things simple, this book will use a simplified naming convention, as follows:

- Pascal casing for classes.

- Camel casing for all methods and variables.

Once you feel comfortable with C# and when you want to know more about the official naming scheme for C#, you may look at <u>Microsoft official naming guidelines</u>.

A FEW THINGS TO REMEMBER WHEN YOU CREATE A SCRIPT (CHECKLIST)

As you create your first scripts, there will be, without a doubt, errors and possibly hair pulling :-). You see, when you start coding, you will, as for any new activity, make small mistakes, learn what they are, improve your coding, and ultimately get better at writing your scripts. As for my previous students, you will make mistakes; these don't make you a bad programmer; on the contrary, it is part of the learning process because we all learn by trial and error, and making mistakes is part of the learning process.

So, as you create your first script, please set any fear aside and try to experiment. Be curious and get to learn the language by practicing. It is like learning a new foreign language: when someone from a foreign country understands your first sentences, you feel so empowered! So, it will be the same with C#, and to ease the learning process, I have included a few tips and things to keep in mind when writing your scripts, so that you progress even faster.

You don't need to know all of these by now (as I will refer to these tips later, in the next chapter), but just be aware of it and also use this list if any error occurs. This list is also available as a pdf file in the resource pack, so that you can print it and keep it close by. So, watch out for these tips :-).

- Each opening bracket has a corresponding closing bracket.

- All variables are written consistently (e.g., spelling and case). The name of each variable is case-sensitive; this means that if you declare a variable **myvariable** but then refer to it as **myVariable** later on in the code, this may trigger an error, as the variables **myVariable** and **myvariable**, because they have a different case (upper- or lower-case **V**), are seen as two different variables.

- None of the local variables have the same name as some of the member variables.

- All variables are declared (type and name) prior to being used (e.g., **int**).

- The type of the argument passed to a method is the type that is required by this method.

- The type of the argument returned by a method is the type that is required to be returned by this method.

- Built-in functions are spelt with the proper case (e.g., upper-case **U** for **Update**).

- Use **Camel casing** (i.e., capitalize the first character of each word except for the first word) or **Pascal casing** (i.e., capitalize the first character of each word) consistently.

- All statements end with a semi-colon ";".

- For **if** statements the condition is within round brackets.

- For **if** statements the condition uses the syntax "==" rather than "=".

- When calling a method, the exact name of this method (i.e., case-sensitive) is used.

- When referring to a variable, it is done with regards to (and awareness of) the access type of the variable (e.g., public or private).

- Local variables are declared and can be used within the same method.

- Member variables are declared outside methods and can be used anywhere within the class.

COMMON ERRORS AND THEIR MEANING

As you will start your journey through C# coding, you may sometimes find it difficult to interpret the errors produced by Unity in the console. However, after some practice, you will manage to recognize them, to understand (and also avoid) them, and to fix them accordingly. The next list identifies the errors that my students often come across when they start coding in C#.

When an error occurs, Unity usually provides you with enough information to check the location of this error in your code, so that you can fix it. While many are relatively obvious to spot, some others are trickier to find. In the following paragraphs, I have listed some of the most common errors that you may come across as you start with C#. The trick is to recognize the error message so that you can understand what Unity is trying to tell you.

Again, this is part of the learning process, and you **WILL** make these mistakes, but as you recognize these errors, you will learn to understand them (and avoid them too :-)).

Again, Unity is trying to help you by communicating, to the best that it can, where the issue is with your code; so by understanding the error messages, we can get to fix these bugs easily. To make it easier to fix errors, Unity usually provides the following information when an error occurs:

- The name of the script where the error was found.

- The location of the error (i.e., row and column).

- A description of the error.

So, if Unity was to generate the following error message…

> **"Assets/Scripts/MyFirstScript.cs (23,34) BCE0085: Unknown identifier: 'localVariable'"**

…it is telling us that an error has occurred in the script called **MyFirstScript**, at the line **23**, and around the **34th** character (or the 34th column) on this line. In this particular message, it is telling us that it can't recognize the variable **localVariable**.

So, you may come across the following errors; this list is also available in the resource pack as a pdf file, so that you can print it and keep it close by:

- **";" expected**: This error could mean that you have forgotten to add a semi-colon at the end of a statement. To fix this error, just go to the line mentioned in the error message and ensure that you add a semi-colon at the end of the statement.

- **Unknown identifier**: This error could mean that Unity does not know the variable that you are mentioning. It can be due to at least three reasons: (1) the variable has not been declared yet, (2) the variable has been declared but outside the scope of the method (e.g., declared locally in a different function), or (3) the name of the variable that you are using is incorrect (i.e., spelling or case). Remember, the names of all variables and functions are case-sensitive; so by just using an incorrect case, Unity will assume that you refer to another variable.

- **The best method overload for function … is not compatible**: This error is probably due to the fact that you are trying to call a function and to pass a list of parameters (which means the number and the types of parameters) that is not compatible with what the function is expecting. For example, the method **mySecondMethod**, described in the next code snippet, is expecting a **String** value for its parameter; so, if you pass an integer value instead, an error will be generated.

```
void mySecondFunction(string name)
{
    print ("Hello, your name is" +name);
}
mySecondFunction("John");//this is correct
mySecondFunction(10);//this will trigger an error
```

- **Expecting } found …:** This error is due to the fact that you may have forgotten to either close or open curly brackets for conditional statements or functions, for example. To avoid this issue, there is a trick (or best practice) that you can use: you can ensure that you indent your code so that corresponding opening and closing brackets are at the same level. In the next example, you can see that the brackets corresponding to the start and the end of the method **testBrackets** are indented at the same level, and so are the brackets for each of the conditional statements within this function. By indenting your code, using several spaces or tabulation, you can make sure that your code is clear and that missing curly brackets are easily spotted.

```
void testBrackets()
{
    if (myVar == 2)
    {
        print ("Hello World");
        myVar = 4;
    }
    else
    {
    }
}
```

Sometimes, although the syntax of your code is correct and does not yield any error in the **Console** window, it looks like nothing is happening; in other words, it looks like the code, and especially the methods that you have created do not work. This is bound to happen as you create your first scripts. It can be quite frustrating (and I have been there :-)) because, in this case, Unity will not let you know where the error is. However, there is a succession of checks that you can perform to ensure that this does not happen; so you could check the following:

- The script that you have written has been saved.

- The script contains no errors.

- The script is attached to an object.

- If the script is indeed attached to an object and you are using a built-in method that depends on the type of object it is attached to, make sure that the script is linked to the correct object. For example, if your script is using the built-in method **OnControllerColliderHit**, which is used to detect collision between the **FPSController** and other objects, but you don't drag and drop the script on the **FPSController** object, the method **OnControllerColliderHit** will not be called if you collide with an object.

- If the script is indeed attached to the right object and is using a built-in method such as **Start**, or **Update**, make sure that these functions are spelt properly (i.e., exact spelling and case). For example, for the method **Update**, the system will call the method **Update** every frame, and no other function. So if you write a method spelt **update**, the system will look for the **Update** function instead, and since it has not been defined (or overwritten), nothing will happen, unless you specifically call this function from your code. The same would happen for the method **Start**. In both cases, the system will assume that you have created two new functions **update** and **start**.

BEST PRACTICES

To ensure that your code is easy to understand and that it does not generate countless headaches when trying to modify it, there are a few good practices that you can start applying as you begin with coding; these should save you some time along the line.

Variable naming

- Use meaningful names that you can understand, especially to those not familiar with your code.

```
string myName = "Patrick";//GOOD
string b = "Patrick";//NOT SO GOOD
```

- Capitalize words within a name consistently (e.g., Camel or Pascal casing).

```
bool testIfTheNameIsCorrect;// GOOD
bool testifthenameiscorrect; // NOT SO GOOD
```

Methods

- Check that all opening brackets have a corresponding closing bracket.

- Indent your code.

- Comment your code as much as possible to explain how it works.

- Use the **Start** method if something just needs to be done once at the start of the scene.

- If something needs to be done repeatedly, then the method **Update** might be a better option.

DEBUGGING USING DICHOTOMY

In addition to providing explanations about your code, you can also use comments to prevent part of your code to be executed. This is very useful when you would like to debug your code and to find where the error or bug might be, using a very simple method called **dichotomy**.

By commenting sections of your code, and by using a process of elimination, you can usually find the issue quickly. For example, you can comment all the code and run the script, then comment half the code, and run the script.

If the code works after this modification, it means that the bug that you are looking for is within the code that has just been commented; otherwise the error is probably in the code that has not yet been commented. Following this modification, we just need to comment half of the portion of the code where you think the error is.

So, by successively commenting more specific areas of our code, you locate the bug relatively quickly. This process is often called **dichotomy** (as we successively divide a code section into two). It is usually very effective to debug your code because the number of iterations (iteratively dividing parts of the code in two) is more predictable and also potentially less time-consuming. For example, for 100 lines of codes, we can successively narrow down the issue to 50, 25, 12, 6, and 3 lines. Between five and six iterations would be necessary in this case compared to checking 100 lines individually.

CREATING A SCRIPT

Now that we have gone through an overview of the best coding practices, it is time to create your first script; so let's get started!

- Please launch Unity.

- Create a new Project (**File | New Project**).

- Create a new scene (**File | New Scene**).

Let's create a new script:

- In the **Project** window, click once on the **Assets** folder.

- Create a new folder where you will be able to store your scripts (this is not compulsory but it will help to organize your scripts) by selecting **Create | Folder** from the **Project** window.

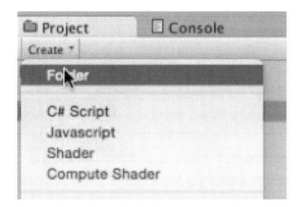

Figure 2-1: Creating a new folder

- This will create a new folder labeled **Folder**.

- Rename this folder **Scripts**.

- Double click on this folder to display its content and so that the script that we are about to create is added to this folder.

- In the **Project** window, select **Create | C# Script**.

- This should create a new **C#** script.

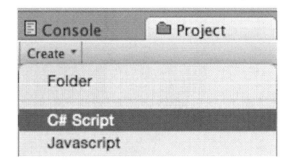

Figure 2-2: Creating a new C# script

- By default, this script will be named **NewBehaviourScript**. However, the name of the script will be highlighted in blue so that you can modify it before its content is created. Please rename this script **Game**.

Note that the name of the script should always match the name of the main class within the script; so if you want to rename this script later, you will also need to modify the name of the main class within the script.

- Click once on the script and look at the **Inspector** window, and you will see the content of the script. By default, you will notice that it includes a definition for the class **Game**, along with namespaces, as well as two different member methods **Start** and **Update**.

- Double-click on the script (within the **Project** window), this will open the script in **MonoDevelop** or **Visual Studio**, depending on the code editor that you have chosen for Unity.

Note that you can select the default code editor used in Unity by modifying Unity's preferences (i.e., **Unity | Preferences | External Tools** for Mac OS or **Edit | Preferences...| External Tools** for Windows).

- The remaining of the examples provided in this book will be using Mono Develop; however, the actions and steps required should be similar if you are using another code editor (e.g., Visual Studio).

- As you open the script, you should see the code that has been generated automatically by Unity. Again, the **Start** method is called at the start of each scene and the method **Update** is called every time the screen is refreshed (that is, every frame).

- These functions are case-sensitive. Because they are built-in functions (i.e., functions made available by Unity for your use), Unity is expecting them to be spelt correctly, otherwise, it will assume that the method that you write serves a different purpose.

WRITING YOUR FIRST STATEMENT

In this section, we will start by coding a simple statement.

So let's start:

- Please open the script called **Game** that you have just created.

- Type the following code inside the **Start** function (new code in bold).

```
void Start()
{

    print ("Hello World");

}
```

- In the previous code, we just create a statement that will print the sentence "**Hello World**" in the **Console** window. As the **Start** function is launched at the start of the scene, this statement should then be executed.

- You can now save your code.

- As your code is saved, you can switch back to Unity and check in the **Console** window for any error messages.

At this stage, when you have checked that the script is error-free, we just need to attach it to an empty object for the code to be executed.

- Please create a new empty object (**GameObject | Create Empty**).

- Rename this object **game**.

- Drag and drop the C# file **Game** from the **Project** window, to the object called **game** in the **Hierarchy**.

- If you click once on the object **game**, you should now see in the **Inspector** that it includes a component called **Game** which is the script that we have just linked to this object.

Now that the script and the object are linked, you can play the scene (**CTRL + P** or **Apple + P**), and you should see the message "**Hello World**" in the **Console** window.

USING VARIABLES

In this section, we will start to use variables and combine them using statements and operators. So let's get started:

- Please add the following code to the **Start** method.

```
//print ("Hello World");
int dateOfBirth = 1990;
int currentYear = 2017;
int age = currentYear - dateOfBirth;
print ("My age is " + age);
```

In the previous code:

- We have commented the previous code using the two forward slashes; so this code will not be executed.

- We declare two variables **dateOfBirth** and **currentYear**.

- We then declare a variable called **age**.

- We perform a subtraction between the variable **currentYear** and the variable **dateOfBirth**, and we then save the result in the variable called **age**.

- Finally, we print the text "**My age is** ", followed by the value of the variable called **age**.

Note that adding a number and a string is equivalent to concatenating these two, so the result of this addition will be a string.

You can now save your code, switch to Unity and play the scene; you should see the message "**My age is 27**" in the **Console** window.

CREATING METHODS

So at this stage we have managed to create two variables and to combine them using the operators + and -, in order to calculate and display the age based on a date of birth and the current year.

In this section, we will get to experiment with methods. So we will create two types of methods: a method that returns no data and that will be used to just display information onscreen, based on a parameter, and a second method that returns the age of an individual calculated using a date of birth and the current year.

So let's get started.

- Please open the script called **Game**.

- Add the following code just after the method **Start** (new code is in bold)

```
void Start ()
{
    //print ("Hello World");
    int dateOfBirth = 1990;
    int currentYear = 2017;
    int age = currentYear - dateOfBirth;
    print ("My age is" + age);
}
void sayHello(string name)
{
    print ("Hello " + name);
}
```

In the previous code:

- We create a method called **sayHello**.

- This method is of type **void**, which means that it does not return any data.

- This method takes one **string** parameter that will be referred to as **name** within the function **sayHello**.

- Within the function **sayHello**, we define what should be done when the function is called: it will print a message onscreen that concatenates the string "**Hello** " and the name passed as a parameter.

The last thing we need to do is to call this method from the **Start** function:

- Please, add the following code to the **Start** function, just after the last **print** statement, as follows (new code in bold).

```
int age = currentYear - dateOfBirth;
print ("My age is" + age);
sayHello("John");
```

In the previous code:

- We call the function **sayHello** and we pass the string **John** as a parameter; so this string will be referred as **name** within the function **sayHello**.

You can now save your code, switch to Unity, and play the scene, and you should see the message "**Hello John**" in the **Console** window.

MODIFYING THE SCOPE OF VARIABLES

In the previous section, we have created variables that were declared within the function **Start**. This means that they are only accessible within this function. As such, they can be called local variables. However, you may want to make these variables accessible throughout your class. For example, we could create a variable called **lastName** that will be seen and used throughout the class as follows:

- Please add the following code at the beginning of the class:

```
string lastName = "Blog";
```

- Modify the function called **sayHello** as follows:

```
void sayHello(string name)
{

    //print ("Hello " + name);

    print ("Hello " + name + " "+ lastName);

}
```

In the previous code, the variable **lastName** is added at the end of the new message.

If you save your code and play the scene, you should see the message "**Hello John**" appear in the **Console** window.

> Note that, in this case, the variable **lastName**, because it is declared outside any method and therefore accessible throughout the class, is called a **member** variable.

CREATING YOUR FIRST CLASS

In the previous section, we created variables and methods. So, at this stage, you should be comfortable with both of these concepts.

We will now start to look at some simple Object-Oriented principles and create our own class. The idea here will be to create a class called **Cube** that will include most of the Object-Oriented concepts that we have seen so far, such as member variables, methods, constructors, and destructors. We will also consider and apply access levels to variables, and we will use other useful structures such as arrays and loops to make our code more efficient.

So let's get started:

- First, from the **Project** view in Unity, create a new C# script and rename it **Cube** (i.e., **Create | C# Script**).

- This class will be used as a template to create objects of type **Cube**.

- Open this script.

- Replace the line

```
public class Cube : Monobehaviour
```

... with this line ...

```
public class Cube
```

- This is because our new class will not extent the **MonoBehaviour** class.

- Add the following lines of code at the beginning of the class (new code in bold).

```
public class Cube
{
    private float speed;
    private int color;
    protected string name;
    private float xPos, yPos, zPos;
```

In the previous code:

- We declare several member variables **speed**, **color**, **name** along with three float variables that will be used for the coordinates of the cube.

- Next, we will create a constructor for this class. As we have seen previously, the constructor will be used when an object of the class **Cube** is instantiated (for example, when a new cube is created).

- Please add the following code within the class **Cube**.

```
public Cube()
{
    speed = 1.0f;
    color = 2;
    name = "Cube";
    xPos = yPos = zPos = 0.0f;
    Debug.Log("I am a new cube and my name is" + name);
}
```

In the previous code:

- We set the values of the member variables **speed**, **color**, and **name**.

- We also set the values of the three **float** variables that will define the position of the **Cube**.

- Lastly, we write the name of the new **Cube** object in the **Console** window.

So at this stage, we have defined the class **Cube**. We have also defined member variables and methods, as well as a constructor for this class. The latter will make it possible to create new **Cubes** from other scripts.

So now, we can start to create a new cube from the script called **Game** as follows:

- Please save the code in the class called **Cube**.

- Open the script called **Game**

- At this stage this script (the script **Game**) should already be linked to an empty object called **game**.

- For clarity, you can, if you wish, comment any of the code that is already present in the functions **Start** or **Update**.

- Add the following code to the **Start** function.

```
Debug.Log ("Creating a new cube");
Cube cube = new Cube ();
```

In the previous code:

- We write the message "**Creating a new cube**" in the **Console** window.

- We also create a new cube by calling its constructor.

- You may notice the syntax:

```
className nameOfVariable = new className ();
```

You can now save your code and play the scene, and you should see the messages "**Creating a new cube**" and "**I am a new cube and my name is Cube**" in the **Console** window.

The reason for the second message is that by writing the following statement …

```
Cube cube = new Cube ();
```

… we effectively call the default constructor from the class **Cube**; and we know that, amongst other things, this constructor will set and display the name of the new **Cube**.

OVERLOADING OUR CONSTRUCTOR

Now that we have created and instantiated a simple class, we will look at the concept of overloading. As you may recall, overloading a method means defining several methods with the same name but with different types of parameters; in our case, we will overload the constructor, so that, at instantiation time (that is, when we create a new object based on our class Cube), we have the choice to call different constructors, each of using different parameters to create a new object.

Overloading is part of the wider concept of polymorphism, where in our case, a method can take several (i.e., "poly") shapes (i.e., "morph").

- Please add the following code to the class called **Cube** (i.e., just before the last curly bracket).

```
public Cube(int newColor)
{
    speed = 1.0f;
    color = newColor;
    name = "Cube";
    xPos = yPos = zPos = 0.0f;


    Debug.Log("I am a new cube and my name is" + name);
    Debug.Log("My Color Number is " + color);
}
```

In the previous code:

- We define a new method called **Cube** that takes an integer parameter that will be referred as **newColor** within this method.

- The member variable **color** is set with the value of the parameter called **newColor**.

- As for the other **Cube** constructor, the member variables **speed**, **name**, **xPos**, **yPos**, and **zPos** are set.

The last thing we need to do now is to modify the call to the constructor in the script called **Game**, so that we instantiate a new **Cube** but using the constructor that we have just defined.

- Please open the script called **Game**.

- Modify it as follows:

```
//Cube cube = new Cube ();
Cube cube2 = new Cube (2);
```

In the previous code:

- We create a new cube called **cube2**.

- We call a constructor and pass the value **2**.

- Because a constructor is called and that an int parameter is passed, then the second constructor (which takes one integer parameter) will be called accordingly.

- As a result, the second constructor is called, and the value **2** should be used to define the color number for the new cube.

Once this is done, you can save both scripts and run the scene. You should see a message saying **"I am a new cube and my name is cube"** followed by **"My Color Number is 2"** in the **Console** window.

USING CONSTANT VARIABLES

In this section, we will be using constant variables; if you remember, constant variables have a constant value; in our case, this will be used to associate a color number to the name of a color so that it is easier to remember and use; so we will be doing the following:

- Define constant variables that will correspond to colors to be used for each of the new cubes.

- Associate each variable with a name.

- Use the constant variable when a cube is created to define its color.

- Display the color of the cube in the **Console** window.

So let's get started:

- Please add the following code at the beginning of the class **Cube**:

```
public const int COLOR_BLUE = 0, COLOR_RED=1, COLOR_YELLOW = 2,
COLOR_GREEN = 3;
```

In the previous code:

- We define four constant variables called **COLOR_BLUE**, **COLOR_RED**, **COLOR_YELLOW**, and **COLOR_GREEN**.

- Each of these colors is associated to a number, respectively **0**, **1**, **2**, and **3**.

- These variables are public which means that they can be accessed from anywhere.

Next, we will create a function that will display the color of our cube; along the way, we will also use a conditional statement.

- Please add the following method to the class **Cube**.

```
public void displayColor()
{
    if (color == COLOR_BLUE)
        Debug.Log ("My Color is blue");
    else Debug.Log ("My color is not blue");
}
```

In the previous code:

- We define a new method called **displayColor**.

- We check whether the color of the cube is blue (that its value is **0**).

- If this is the case, we then print the message "**My Color is Blue**".

- Otherwise, we print the message "**My color is not blue**".

At this stage we just need to modify the script called **Game** so that we can create a new cube based on a constant variable (for the color of the cube) and display this color also.

- Please open the script called **Game**.

- Add the following code to the **Start** function.

```
Cube cube3 = new Cube (Cube.COLOR_BLUE);
cube3.displayColor ();
```

In the previous code:

- We create a new Cube variable called **cube3**.

- We call the second constructor, passing an integer variable; however, this time, we use a constant variable (as it is easier to remember) to define its color.

- We use the constant variable **Cube.COLOR_BLUE** to define the color of this cube. This is made possible because the variable **COLOR_BLUE**, although it belongs to the class **Cube**, is public, which means that we can access it from anywhere.

- We use the constant variable **Cube.COLOR_BLUE** as a parameter; you may note that the variable **COLOR.BLUE** could have been used without the need to instantiate a new cube.

- We then call the method **displayColor** (which is public) to display the color of the cube.

You can now save your code and play the scene, and the console window should display the message saying **"I am a new cube and my name is cube"** followed by **"My Color Number is blue"**.

CONSTANT AND STATIC VARIABLES

In the previous section, we have used constant variables to define the colors of the cubes that we have created. We could also have used static variables instead as these variables share similarities; however, they also differ in several ways:

- Both static and constant variables are shared across instances of the same class.

- Constant variables cannot be changed after they have been declared whereas static variable can be modified afterwards.

- Constant variables cannot be set in a function, whereas static variables can.

USING THE SWITCH CASE STRUCTURE

In this section we will use some interesting structures to make our code more efficient.

As we have seen in the previous section, we used the function **displayColor** to display the color of a cube; to do so, we used a conditional statement to test the value of the color before displaying it in the **Console** window.

You may notice that if we wanted to test the four different colors, we would use four different conditional statements, but that may be unnecessary. Instead, we could use the **switch case** structure; if you remember, this structure allows to go to a specific part of the code based on the value of an integer; so we could use a **switch** structure to display a message that depends on the color of a cube.

So let's get started:

- Please add the following code to the script **Cube**.

```
public void displayColor2()
{
    switch (color)
    {
        case COLOR_BLUE: {Debug.Log ("My Color is
blue");break;}
        case COLOR_RED: {Debug.Log ("My COlor is red");break;}
        case COLOR_YELLOW: {Debug.Log ("My COlor is
yellow");break;}
        case COLOR_GREEN: {Debug.Log ("My COlor is
green");break;}
    default: break;
    }
}
```

In the previous code:

- We define a public method called **displayColor2**.

- We then create a switch structure based on the variable color; in other words: we will switch to a particular branch of our code based on the value of the variable **color**.

- In our case, if the variable color equals to the value of the variable **COLOR_BLUE**, we write the message **"My Color is blue"**. In this particular case, all the instructions are written within curly brackets (although this is not compulsory), and the last instruction is **break**; this means that after displaying the message in the **Console** window, we will exit the switch structure; this ensures that all branches in the switch structure are mutually exclusive; in other words, we will use **branch 1**, **branch 2** or **branch 3**, but we won't be going through more than one branch at a time.

- We proceed in a similar way for the colors red, yellow, and green.

- The switch structure ends with the code:

```
default:break;
```

- This means that if none of the branches have been executed, this **default** branch will be executed and we will then exit the switch loop.

You can now save your code. We will be testing it in the next section; however, if you'd like to perform a test now, you could just to modify the **Game** class as follows:

```
//cube3.displayColor().;
cube3.displayCOlor2();
```

USING ARRAYS AND LOOPS

To be able to test the switch structure that we have created in the previous section, we will start to create four different boxes, each with a different color.

- Please add the following code to the script called **Game** in the **Start** function.

```
Cube[] cubes = new Cube[4];
for (int i = 0; i <= 3; i++)
{
        cubes [i] = new Cube (i);
        cubes [i].displayColor2 ();
}
```

In the previous code:

- We create an array of cubes; this array will include four **Cubes**.

- We then create a loop that goes from 0 to 3 using an increment of 1 (that is: 0, 1, 2, and 3).

- Within this loop, we define each **Cube** that belong to the array called **cubes**.

- For each of these **Cubes** we call the second constructor of the class and pass the value of the variable called **i** (i.e., 0, 1, 2, or 3) to define the color of the cube.

- When this is done, we call the member method **displayColor2** for each of these cubes, so that the corresponding color is displayed.

Now that this is done, and to be able to see the corresponding messages in the **Console** window, you can comment the following code in the **Game** script.

```
//Cube cube = new Cube ();
//Cube cube2 = new Cube (2);
//cube.displayColor ();
//Cube cube3 = new Cube (Cube.COLOR_BLUE);
//cube3.displayColor ();
```

You can also comment the following line in the first constructor of the class **Cube**.

```
//Debug.Log("My Color Number is " + color);
```

You can now save your code and play the scene; you should see the following messages in the **Console** window: **"My Color is Blue"**, **"My Color is red"**, **"My Color is yellow"**, and **"My Color is green"**.

Now that this is working, there is a last thing that we could do to simplify our code: instead of using the switch loop, we could, instead, use an array of string variables that define the color of each of the cubes.

Let's see how this can be done:

- Please add the following code at the start of the class **Cube**.

```
private string [] colors = {"BLUE", "RED", "YELLOW", "GREEEN"};
```

In the previous code, we define an array of string values called **colors** and we also initialize this array with the corresponding strings values.

- Please add the following method to the class called **Cube**.

```
public void displayColor3()
{
    Debug.Log("My Color is "+colors[color]);
}
```

In the previous code:

- We define a public method called **displayColor3**.

- In this method we display the color of the current cube.

- To do so, we use the member variable **color** as an index to select the corresponding string in the array called **colors**. For for example, if we have created a blue cube, its member variable color should be equal to **0**; so, the corresponding string would be located at the index 0 in the array called **colors**, which corresponds to the string **"BLUE"**.

- The same applies to the other colors; the key here is to ensure that, when you define the array called **colors**, you check that the order of the strings in the array (for example **BLUE** or **RED**) corresponds to the name of the colors defined for the constant variables **COLOR_BLUE** (i.e., 0), **COLOR_RED** (i.e., 1) and so on and so forth.

Last but not least, you can modify the script **Game** as follows (new code in bold) so that the new function called **displayColor3** is called instead of **displayColor2**:

```
for (int i = 0; i <= 3; i++)
{
        cubes [i] = new Cube (i);

        //cubes [i].displayColor2 ();

        cubes [i].displayColor3 ();
}
```

After making these changes, you can save your code and play the scene; you should see the following messages in the **Console** window **"My Color is BLUE"**, **"My Color is RED"**, **"My Color is YELLOW"**, and **"My Color is GREEN"**.

So as you can see, there are many ways to combine conditional statements, loops, and arrays to be able to optimize your code.

INSTANTIATING VISUAL OBJECTS IN YOUR SCENE

So far, the objects that we have created did not have any corresponding visual object in the scene view. So in this section, we will instantiate a new cube onscreen that corresponds to the cube that we have created in our script. This will be an interesting way to tie-in the concepts that we have looked at so far with Unity objects and primitives; we will also use the concept of inheritance.

So we will do the following:

- Create a new constructor for the class **Cube** that accounts for the name, the position and the color of the cube; this is so that new cubes can be easily identified in the **Scene** view.

- Create a new class called **VisualCube** that inherits from the class **Cube**.

- Modify this new class so that, in addition to the member methods and variables inherited from its parent, this class creates a visual representation of the cube in the **Scene** view, based on its position, its color, and its name.

So let's get started:

- Please open the script called **Cube**.

- Add the following code at the beginning of the class.

```
protected Vector3 position;
```

In the previous code:

- We declare a **Vector3** variable called **position**.

- This variable is protected, which means that it will be accessible from the class **Cube** and its children.

Once this is done, we will create a new class called **VisualCube** as follows:

- Please create a new C# script called **VisualCube**.

- Open this script.

- Modify the first line as follows:

```
public class VisualCube : Cube {
```

In the previous code:

- We declare a new class called **VisualCube**, and we specify that it inherits from the class called **Cube**.

- This means that it will inherit all its member methods (including the constructors) and member variables (for example, the variable **color**).

Next we will create a new constructor for this class. This constructor will be partially based on its parent, but it will also include some additional and more interesting features.

- Please add the following code to the class.

```
public VisualCube(int newColor, Vector3 newPosition, string
newName): base(newColor)
{

    name = newName;

    position = newPosition;

    GameObject g =
GameObject.CreatePrimitive(PrimitiveType.Cube);

    g.name = name;

    g.transform.position = position;

}
```

In the previous code:

- We define a constructor for our new class.

- The constructor will take three parameters: an int (the variable **color**), a Vector3 (the variable **newPosition**) and a string (the variable **newName**).

- When the constructor is called, it will first call the constructor from the parent class (or the **base** class) and pass the parameter **newColor** to this constructor. This is performed thanks to the following code:

```
: base(newColor)
```

So by using this syntax, we use the constructor from the base class and also include additional features.

- Then, we define the name of the cube as well as its position.

- We create a new primitive (which is a cube) in the **Scene** view with the corresponding name and at the corresponding position.

Next, we just need to use this class in the script called **Game**.

- Please add the following code at the end of the **Start** function in the script called **Game**.

```
VisualCube [] vCubes = new VisualCube [4];
for (int i = 0; i <= 3; i++)
{
      vCubes [i] = new VisualCube (i, new
Vector3(0.0f,i*1.0f,0.0f), "Cube"+i);
}
```

In the previous code:

- We create an array of **VisualCube** objects.

- We then create a loop.

- In this loop, each element of the array **vCubes** is instantiated, and we specify a new position and a new name for each of these objects through the constructor.

As you play the scene, you will see that you have created four cubes in the **Scene** view, named **Cube0**, **Cube1**, **Cube2**, and **Cube3**, as per the next figures.

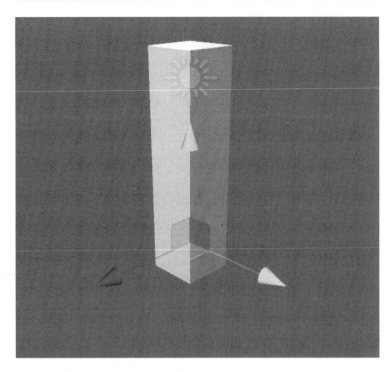

Figure 3: Creating VisualCube objects

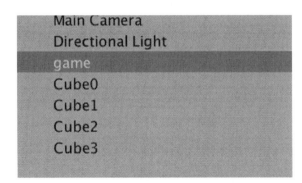

Figure 4: The VisualCube objects in the Hierarchy window

The last thing we could do is to allocate a color to all of these cubes.

- Please open the script called **VisualCube**.

- Add the following code at the end of the constructor.

```
switch (newColor)
{
     case Cube.COLOR_BLUE:       {g.GetComponent<Renderer>
().material.SetColor("_Color", Color.blue);break;}

     case Cube.COLOR_RED:  {g.GetComponent<Renderer>
().material.SetColor("_Color", Color.red);break;}

     case Cube.COLOR_YELLOW:       {g.GetComponent<Renderer>
().material.SetColor("_Color", Color.yellow);;break;}

     case Cube.COLOR_GREEN:        {g.GetComponent<Renderer>
().material.SetColor("_Color", Color.green);break;}

     default: break;
}
```

In the previous code:

- As we have done in the past sections, we use a switch structure where we go to a specific branch based on the value of the variable **newColor**.

- In each case, we access the **Renderer** component of the new object, and we then access its **material** attribute.

- We then set the color of the **Cube** depending on the variable **newColor**.

If you save your code and run the scene, you should see, as illustrated in the next figure, four boxes, each with a different color, in the **Game** and **Scene** views.

Figure 5: Four boxes created from code

LEVEL ROUNDUP

Well, this is it!

In this chapter, we have learned about some interesting Object Oriented concepts. We have created a class, along with a combination of variables, methods, loops and conditional statements. Along the way, we also used the concepts of constructors, overloading, overriding, and inheritance to create a new class called **VirtualCube** that inherited from the class **Cube** and that made it possible to display a cube onscreen based on its color. So, we have, again, covered some significant ground compared to the last chapter.

Checklist

You can consider moving to the next chapter if you can do the following:

- Create your own class.

- Create member variables and methods.

- Create a constructor that partially utilizes the constructor from the base class.

Quiz

Now, let's check your knowledge! Please answer the following questions or specify if these statements are either correct or incorrect (the solutions are on the next page).

1. In C# two member methods can have the same name.

2. When a variable is protected it can only be accesses from the base class.

3. When a variable is private it can only be accesses from the base class.

4. A **switch case** structure is similar to using if statements.

5. An array is better suited for data sets that don't expand overtime.

6. Lists are better used for data sets that expand overtime.

7. In **Dictionaries**, each item can be accessed through its key.

8. A class can have several constructors.

9. Constructors have the same name as their class.

10. Overloading a constructor makes it possible to pass different parameters when a class is instantiated.

Quiz Solutions

Now, let's check if you have answered the questions correctly.

1. True (as long as the list and types of the parameters are different).

2. False.

3. True.

4. True.

5. True.

6. True.

7. True.

8. True.

9. True.

10. True.

Challenge 1

Now that you have managed to complete this chapter and that you have created your first class, you can do the following:

- Create a class called student based on the following code.

```
public class Student
{


    public string firstName;

    public string lastName;

    public Student(string fName, string lName)

    {

        firstName = fName;

        lastName = lName;

    }

}
```

In the script called **Game**:

- Create a dictionary of students

- Use their id as a key.

- Display the name of one of the students based on its id.

3

INTRODUCTION TO LINEAR ALGEBRA WITH C# FOR UNITY

In this section, we will look at some linear algebra concepts and see how they can be applied in Unity through C#, including:

- Referential and vectors (i.e., 2D and 3D).

- Norm, normalizing, or direction.

- Performing operations on vectors (for example, additions, subtractions, and products) and how these can be used in your own games.

- Using vectors to improve the gameplay (for example, using dot products).

So, after completing this chapter, you will be able to:

- Understand how vectors work and when and why they need to be used in games.

- Combine vectors in C#.

- Perform simple operations on vectors using C#.

> The code solutions for this chapter are included in the **resource pack** that you can download by following the instructions included in the section entitled "Support and Resources for this Book".

USING VECTORS AND FORCES

Throughout your learning with Unity, and although you may not initially like algebra, you will find it very useful to understand some basic concepts linked to vectors and operations on vectors. If these names sound exotic to you or have given you a headache in the past, not to worry, they will be explained in depth and clearly in relation to Unity so that you can gain a clearer understanding of their application in the context of game development with Unity. If you ever wondered, for instance, how NPCs can detect you in the game Half-Life, and how wind can be simulated in a game, then this section should be very useful. After completing this chapter you will be able to:

- Understand basic mathematical concepts such as scalars and vectors.

- Understand how they can be used in Unity in both the **Scene** view and through coding.

- Apply some simple mathematical operations involving vectors, and understand how they are applied in games.

More importantly, you will understand how these concepts relate to your game development, including for the following features:

- **Detecting when the player is entering an NPC's field of view:** Adding sensory detection to your NPC always adds realism to your game as the NPCs behave as if they were actually seeing (and reacting to) the player. This is the case in games such as Half-Life where NPCs start to shoot at the player when s/he enters their Field of View (FOV).

- **Helping NPCs to detect whether the player is close:** In addition to visual sensory detection, you can also improve your game by simulating the detection of sounds, based on distance. For example, in several games, the NPCs, even if you walk behind them, will detect you if you are within a specific radius, and this can be calculated thanks to vectors (by calculating the magnitude or the Euclidian distance). In games like **Unreal Tournament**, the damage inflicted by many types of weapons can also depend on the distance between protagonists; for example, if you use a weapon that is very powerful at close range, the opponent could sustain serious injuries.

- **Simulating wind forces**: Forces are very important in games. Games based on gravity (for example, the game **Worms**), or pool games, rely on the accurate application of forces to increase realism. In pool games, for example, the direction and speed of the colored ball will usually depend on the speed and direction of the white ball, and all of these parameters (such as direction or speed) are usually expressed as vectors.

As you can see, vectors and linear algebra can play an important role in making your game more realistic by improving the Artificial Intelligence and by making sure that the objects in the game behave in a realistic way (that is, that they follow the laws of physics).

COORDINATE SYSTEMS

In Unity, because objects are displayed in either 2D or 3D, we need a system to be able to locate them easily and unambiguously. For this purpose, a coordinate system is used to provide each object with unique attributes that make it possible to locate them. In Unity, we use a **Cartesian** coordinate system (which is named after the French philosopher and mathematician **René Descartes**), which gives a set of coordinates to an object along arbitrarily-defined axes. When we deal with two-dimensional or three-dimensional objects, for example (for example, for the user interface), we use the coordinates x and y. We know that if two objects have the same x and y coordinates in a two-dimensional Cartesian system, they will then be at the same position.

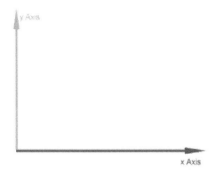

Figure 6: A two-dimensional coordinate system

However, for 3D environments, we add another coordinate called z, which provides the notion of depth. So, in a three-dimensional space, an object would ideally have three coordinates to determine its location: x, y and z. The x-, y-, and z-axes are perpendicular to each other; if the positive x-axis points to the right, and the positive y-axis points upwards, then the positive z-axis points towards us, in the case of a **right-handed coordinate system**, and outwards in the case of a **left-handed coordinate system**.

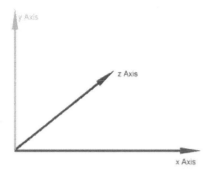

Figure 7: A three-dimensional coordinate system

Unity employs a left-handed coordinate system; so when the positive x is pointing to the right, and the positive y-axis is pointing upwards, the positive z-axis is pointing outwards, as illustrated in the next figure.

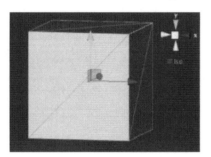

Figure 8: The three-dimensional coordinate system used in Unity

As we can see in the previous figure, the positive x-axis (i.e., the red axis on the previous figure) is pointing to the right, the positive y-axis (i.e., the green axis on the previous figure) is pointing upwards, and the positive z-axis (i.e., the blue axis on the previous figure) is pointing outwards.

This is called a left-handed coordinate system because we can use our left hand to determine the orientation of the resulting cross product of (i.e., the axis perpendicular to) the x- and y-axes using our left hand: if we point our thumb to the right (x-axis), and our index upwards, the middle finger is pointing outwards (z-axis). Given that we have defined the x and y axes as two perpendicular axes, the z-axis will also be defined as the cross product of these two (that is, perpendicular to both the x- and the y-axis).

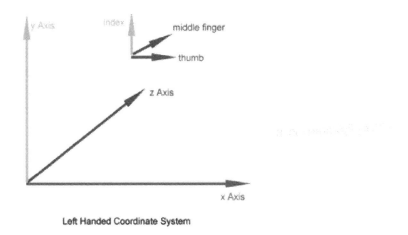

Left Handed Coordinate System

Figure 9: A left-handed coordinate system

Based on the previous diagram, we can also see that the orientation for the positive z-axis will be different if we use the right hand (that is, the opposite direction). In this case, the z-axis will be pointing towards us.

SCALARS AND VECTORS

So far, even if you are not used to vectors, you may already have used float, int, or Boolean variables to define a quantity. If you were, let's say, observing a moving object, determining its speed could be done using a float (for example 3.2 meters per second). However, this quantity, often referred as a magnitude, would not provide any information on the direction of the object (that is, where the object is going). For example, an object could be going a 3.2 meters per second towards the positive or negative x-axis. So while having the magnitude is useful, knowing the direction of the movement is even more important to determine where this object is going. When we combine the magnitude of the speed to its direction, we obtain the velocity, a vector representation that includes information about both the speed and the direction of that object.

WHY USE VECTORS RATHER THAN SCALARS?

The advantage of using a vector is that not only can you specify a value for a particular attribute of an object, but you can also specify a direction, which is very important when we deal with two-dimensional or three-dimensional games, that will more than likely include moving objects.

Using vectors makes it possible to apply transformations to these objects for their animation, and to also determine additional information such as speed or acceleration.

For example, in physics, when we know the acceleration vector of an object, we can, based on successive operations (known as integrations and derivations) determine their speed and position overtime, which makes it possible to create a realistic simulation that mirrors their movement in real life (for example, a canon ball subject to gravity).

MATHEMATICAL NOTATIONS FOR VECTORS

Vectors, in addition to their magnitude, also have a direction. They can be used to specify a position or forces for example. Vectors are usually expressed in two or three dimensions and their coordinates are broken down for each direction (or axis) of the coordinate system in use (that is, along the x-, y-, and z-axes for a three dimensional Cartesian coordinate system).

Unity is using a Cartesian coordinate system, which means that vector coordinates are expressed using two or three attributes. Each of these attributes corresponds to the projection of a vector on one of the two or three axes, respectively, that make up the Cartesian coordinate system.

For example, the velocity of an object could be described as follows in a three-dimensional Cartesian system.

$$\vec{v} = v_x \vec{x} + v_y \vec{y} + v_z \vec{z}$$

The arrows above v, x, y, and z specify that we are not dealing with a scalar (value) but a quantity that also has a direction (i.e., a vector). A scalar would always be numerical and would not have a direction (but vectors do).

This means that the coordinates of the velocity are **Vx**, **Vy**, and **Vz**. Vx is the x coordinate for the vector V. In other words, when you look at the coordinates of the vector, it will have three parameters: x, y, and z. So Vx will be the x coordinate, Vy the y coordinate and Vz corresponds to the z coordinate.

$\vec{x}, \vec{y}$ and $\vec{z}$ are called unit vectors because their magnitude is 1 and because each of them points towards the positive x-, y- and z-axes, respectively.

A vector can be noted in different formats including:

$$\vec{v} = \begin{bmatrix} v_x \\ v_y \\ v_z \end{bmatrix} \text{ or } \vec{v} = \begin{bmatrix} v_x & v_y & v_z \end{bmatrix}$$

The magnitude of a vector (often referred as its **Euclidean length**) can be noted and calculated as follows:

$$|v| = \sqrt{v_x^2 + v_y^2 + v_z^2}$$

Since the coordinates of the vector are all projections of this vector in the three axes, and that these are at right angles, Pythagoras's theorem can help to determine the magnitude.

Unit vectors have a magnitude of 1. It is often necessary to normalize a vector (i.e., to ensure that their norm is 1), as we will see later on. This means that the vector keeps its direction while its magnitude is reduced to 1.

In 3D scenes, 3D vectors are used for information such as position or transformations, including scaling or rotating. This is the case for any 3D object added to your scene. When looking at its properties in the **Inspector**, you will notice a **Transform** attribute. This transform, in turn, provides information on the position, rotation, and scale of this object, as described in the next figure.

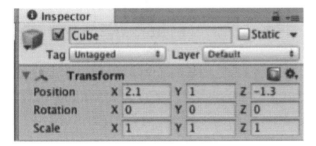

Figure 10: Transforms in Unity

In the previous figure, you can see that the object labelled **Cube** includes a **Transform** attribute and additional properties such as *position*, *rotation*, and *scale*, all expressed using three coordinates. For example, on the previous figure, we can see that the object's position is (2.1, 1, -1.3), that its rotation is (0, 0, 0) and that its scale is (1, 1, 1).

In Unity, the rotation attributes determine the amount of rotation around the x-, y-, and z axis. The scale attributes indicate by how much the object is scaled along the x-, y- and z-axes.

USING VECTORS IN UNITY

Unity provides several built-in classes to create and manipulate vectors: the classes **Vector2** and **Vector3**. Generally, 2D vectors are used for 2D scenes and 3D vectors are used for 3D scenes.

For example, if you were to create a vector in C#, you could do so as follows:

```
Vector2 velocity = new Vector2 (2,0);
```

In this code, we declare a vector of type **Vector2**. This code could be used to describe a velocity of 2 meters per second, along the x-axis going towards the positive x values.

In a similar way, we could also declare a 3D vector as follows:

```
Vector3 velocity = new Vector3 (2,0,0);
```

This code could be used to describe a velocity of 2 meters per second, along the x-axis going towards the positive x values. As we will see later, you can perform many operations on vectors (such as addition, subtraction, dot product or cross product), and these mathematical operations can also be performed through the built-in **Vector2** and **Vector3** classes.

PERFORMING OPERATIONS ON VECTORS

Additions, subtractions, or more complex operations such as cross products, can be performed on vectors.

Adding and subtracting vectors

One of the most basic operations is to add or subtract vectors. This can be useful to determine the position of an object based on two other objects. It can also be used to add forces and to calculate the net force applied to an object. For example, let's consider two vectors **a** and **b** defined as follows:

$$\vec{a} = a_x\vec{x} + a_y\vec{y} + a_z\vec{z}$$

and

$$\vec{b} = b_x\vec{x} + b_y\vec{y} + b_z\vec{z}$$

Then the sum the two vectors is defined as follows:

$$\vec{c} = \vec{a} + \vec{b}$$

$$\vec{c} = c_x\vec{x} + c_y\vec{y} + c_z\vec{z}$$

where:

$$c_x = a_x + b_x$$
$$c_Y = a_Y + b_Y$$
$$c_z = a_z + b_z$$

ADDING VECTORS IN UNITY

You may need to add vectors in your games to simulate forces applied in different directions. You may need an object to be subject to wind forces coming from different directions and to calculate and apply the net force accordingly. To be able to do so, you will need to determine these forces as vectors, add them to obtain the resulting net force, and then apply this net force to a solid. The following diagram shows how a vector called **V3** can be created by adding two other vectors **V1** and **V2**.

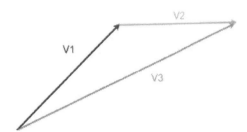

Figure 11: Adding two vectors

In the previous figure, we can see that going from the tail to the head of the vector **V3** is the same as following the vector **V1** and then the vector **V2**.

The following code could be added to an object that has a **RigidBody** component. A **RigidBody** component will ensure that, amongst other things, forces can be applied to this object in Unity.

```
Vector3 v1, v2, v3;
void Start ()
{
  v1 = new Vector3 (0,0,1);
  v2 = new Vector3 (1,0,0);
  v3 = v1+v2;
}
void FixedUpdate ()
{
  GetComponent<Rigidbody>().AddForce(v3*10);
}
```

In the previous code:

- We declare three vectors.

- We initialize the two vectors that will represent the forces applied to the object.

- We add the two vectors (forces) and calculate the resulting vector (that is, the net force).

- We multiply the net force by 10 and apply it to the object.

Based on our previous explanation on adding vectors, the vector V3 should have the coordinates (1=0+1, 0=0+0, 1=1+0) and the force applied should have the coordinates (10=10*1, 10=10*1, 10=10*1).

MULTIPLYING VECTORS BY SCALARS

In addition to additions and subtractions, it is also possible to multiply a vector by a scalar (i.e., a number). In this case, and while the vector will preserve its direction, its magnitude will be changed (i.e., multiplied by the scalar). In the following example, we use two vectors: the initial vector **V1,** and the vector **V2** which represents **V1** multiplied by **2**.

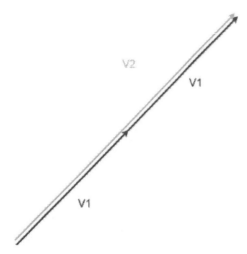

Figure 12: Multiplying a vector by a scalar

$$\vec{v} = \begin{bmatrix} v_x \\ v_y \\ v_z \end{bmatrix}$$

$$\vec{v'} = 2\vec{v} = 2\begin{bmatrix} v_x \\ v_y \\ v_z \end{bmatrix} = \begin{bmatrix} 2v_x \\ 2v_y \\ 2v_z \end{bmatrix}$$

On the previous figure, you may see that the first vector has a sign that looks like a quote '. This means **prime**, so we are talking about another vector than v that is called **v prime** (but you can use a different name if you wish), which is twice the vector v.

In Unity, multiplying a vector is also quite simple and it can be done as follows:

```
Vector3 v1 = new Vector3 (1,1,1);
Vector3 v2 = 2 * v1;
```

In the previous code:

- We declare a new vector.

- We multiply the vector v1 by 2 and we should obtain a vector with the coordinates (2, 2, 2).

USING DOT PRODUCTS

As many other game developers, you may be creating a game where you would like to be able to detect when the player is in the field of view of an NPC. So, how can we, using simple mathematics, determine when the player will enter the NPC's field of view, as illustrated in the next figure?

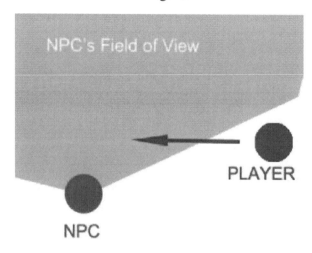

Figure 13: AI detection: overview

To solve this problem, we can use a concept called **dot product** to determine whether the angle between the direction of the NPC and the vector between the NPC and the player.

The Maths

The definition of a dot product between two vectors is the product of their magnitude multiplied by the cosine of the angle between these vectors. In practical terms, we multiply the two vectors. However, to do so, we need to consider whether they are in the same direction. So the cosine will provide us with the projection of one of the vectors on the other one and we can then multiply this projection by the magnitude of the other vector.

The dot product effectively tells us about the angle between these vectors and to what extent they are aligned. For example, a positive dot product indicates that the angle between the two vectors is between -90 and 90 degrees, and a null dot product indicates that they are perpendicular to each-other. The formula to calculate a dot product is as follows:

dotProduct = |v1|+|v2|*cos(alpha)

- Alpha refers to the angle between the two vectors.

- The two bars || around v1 and v2 refer to the norm of the vectors (i.e., their length).

Some of the built-in classes available in Unity make it easier to use the dot product, as demonstrated in the next code snippet:

```
Vector3 v1 = new vector (1,1,1);
Vector3 v2 = new vector (-2,-2,-2);
float productOfV1AndV2 = Vector3.Dot(v1,v2);
```

In the previous code:

- The vector v1 is created.

- The vector v2 is created.

- The dot product of these vectors is calculated.

- In this case, the dot product is -2; so we know that the angle between the vectors is between 90 and 270 degrees.

It would be great, however, to know more about the direction of these vectors, and more importantly if they are aligned or pointing in the same direction. For this purpose, we can normalize these vectors first (that is, reduce their magnitude to 1). This way, if they point in the exact same direction, the dot product will be 1; and if they are in the opposite direction, the dot product will be -1. This is because when we calculate the dot product, if the magnitudes of both vectors are 1, the dot product will be equal to the cosine of the angle between these two. Because the cosine is equal to one if the angle is 0 and -1 if the angle is 180, it is now easier to check if these vectors are aligned. In Unity, we could do this as follows:

```
Vector3 v1 = new Vector3 (1,1,1);
Vector3 v2 = new Vector3 (-2,-2,-2);
float productOfV1AndV2 = Vector3.Dot(v1.normalized,v2.
normalized);
```

In the previous code:

- The first two lines are similar to the previous code.

- We calculate the dot product of these vectors; in this case, we will find that the dot product equals **-1**, which means that the vectors are pointing in opposite directions.

Solution

To answer our initial question, we could do as follows:

- If we call the field of view alpha, knowing whether the NPC is in the field of view is equivalent to know whether the angle determined by the direction of the NPC (V1 on the next diagram) and the vector that points towards the player from the NPC (V2 in the next diagram) is comprised between -alpha/2 and alpha/2. So for a field of view of 90 degrees, the angle defined by V1 and V2 should be comprised between -45 degrees and +45 degrees. This is explained on the next diagram: if we imagine the vector V2 rotating counterclockwise, if V2 enters the green zone, then we know that the player is in the field of view.

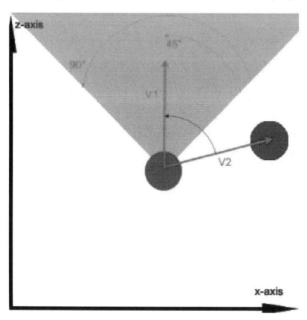

Figure 14: Key variables to detect the player

- So as described on the previous diagram, and knowing that Cosine (45) is approximately 0.7, that Cosine (0) is 1, and that Cosine (-45) is approximately also 0.7, we know that the player is in the field of view if the angle between V1 and V2 is between -45° and +45° or, in a similar way, if the Cosine of the angle between the vectors V1 and V2 is comprised between 0.7 and 1.

- This is because when the player is on the right border of the field of view, the angle between V1 and V2 is -45° (Cosine = 0.7)

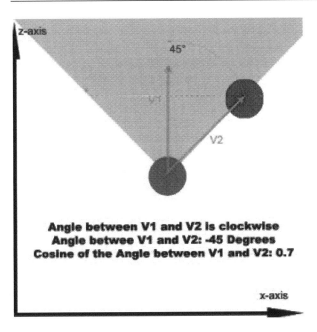

Figure 15: The player enters the FOV (right side)

- When the player is in front of the NPC, the angle between V1 and V2 is 0 (Cosine = 1)

- When the player is on the left border of the field of view, the angle between V1 and V2 is 45° (Cosine = 0.7). So effectively, when the NPC is in the field of view, the Cosine of the angle will vary between 0.7 and 1.

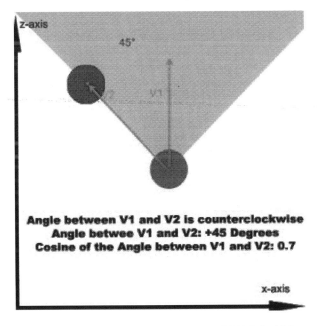

Figure 16: The player is about to exit the FOV (left side)

- We have arbitrarily chosen 90° to simulate the horizontal field of view for some humans, but you could, if you wished, increase it to 100°.

Now that we have clarified the calculation of the cosine, let's explain how we can find the vectors V1 and V2. V1 is the forward direction for the NPC. This vector originates (on the diagram) from the NPC and is going in the direction of the positive z-axis. V2 is determined by the position of both the NPC and the player.

Let's see how: as you can see on the next diagram, the vectors V2, Vnpc and Vplayer form a triangle. Vnpc is the vector for the position of the NPC and it starts at the origin of the coordinate system. Vplayer is the vector for the position of the NPC and, as for the previous vector, it starts at the origin of the coordinate system. If we operate a clockwise loop from the origin of the coordinate system, we can go from the origin of the coordinate system to the NPC by following the vector Vnpc, then follow the vector V2 (from its tail to its head), and then follow the vector Vplayer in reverse (that is, from its head to its tail; this is the same as **-Vplayer**) to be back to the origin of the coordinate system. So we could say that: **Vnpc + V2-Vplayer = 0**; in other words, by following Vnpc, then V2, and then Vplayer in reverse, we end up at the same point. Following this, we can then say that: **V2 = -Vnpc + Vplayer** (we just added -V2 to both sides of the previous equation) and this is how we can calculate V2.

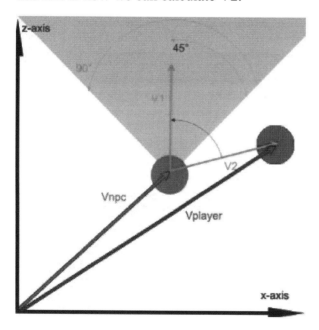

Figure 17: Calculating V1 and V2

So at this stage, we know V1 and V2 and we just need to calculate the dot product between these vectors to have an idea of the cosine of the resulting angle between these vectors. However, if you remember the definition of a dot product, the cosine of this angle equals the dot product only if the magnitude of the vectors is 1, or in other words, if these vectors have been normalized. Normalizing can be done easily in Unity as each vector can access the function/method called **normalized** which returns a normalized version accordingly.

At this stage, we have two normalized vectors V1 and V2 (each of magnitude 1) and we need to calculate the cosine of the angle between them. You will notice that, so far, we have been using degrees for angles (FOV=90°). However, the function that calculates the cosine in Unity only takes radians (and not degrees) as parameters. So we will need to convert our angle in radians first before the cosine can be calculated. This can be done using the function **Mathf.Deg2Rad** in Unity.

Now we have an angle expressed in radians and we can calculate the dot product of the normalized versions of V1 and V2. That's great! Bearing in mind that when the player is on the right border of the field of view, the angle between V1 and V2 is -45° (Cosine = 0.7), that when the player is in front of the NPC the angle between V1 and V2 is 0 (Cosine = 1), and that when the player is on the left border of the field of view the angle between V1 and V2 is 45° (Cosine = 0.7), we effectively know that for the NPC to detect the player (or the player to enter the Field of View of the NPC), the cosine of the angle between V1 and V2 should be comprised between 0.7 and 1.

So to implement this method through C# code, we could do the following:

- Create two objects (boxes) and rename them respectively **player** and **NPC**.

- Move the **player** object at the position **(3, 0, 1)** using the **Inspector**.

- Move the **NPC** object at the position **(0, 0, 0)** using the **Inspector**.

- Create a new C# script (from the **Project** window, select **Create | C# Script**).

- Name this script **DetectPlayer**.

- Drag and drop the script on the **NPC** object.

- Open this script and type the following code:

```
float field_of_view;

float minCosine;

float dotP; //dot product of v1 and v2


void Start()

{

    FOVInDegrees = 90;

    FOVInRadians = FOVInDegrees*Mathf.Deg2Rad;

    minCosine = Mathf.Cos(FOVInRadians/2);

}

void Update()

{

    //We draw rays at a 45-and +45 degree angles in green from
the NPC to highlight the field of view

    //Quaternions are used to rotate the direction of the rays
around the y axis; the length of each ray is 10

    //These rays are only visible in the scene view (not the game
view)

    Debug.DrawRay(transform.position, Quaternion.Euler
(0,45,0)*Vector3.forward*10,Color.green, 10);

    Debug.DrawRay(transform.position, Quaternion.Euler (0,-
45,0)*Vector3.forward*10,Color.green, 10);


    //We draw a ray for v1 (direction of the NPC) using the same
principle

    Debug.DrawRay(transform.position, Vector3.forward, Color.red,
10);


    //all necessary vectors are defined

    v_npc = transform.position;

    v_player = GameObject.Find ("player").transform.position;

    v1 = new Vector3(0,0,1);//the NPC looks forward
```

```
    v2 = v_player - v_npc;//v2 calculated as formula specified
previously


    //we use normalized versions of the vectors to obtain the
Cosine and compare it with the min cosine

    //this serves to determine the angle between V1 and V2, and
ultimately to determine whether the player is in the field of
view

    dotP = Vector3.Dot(v1.normalized,v2.normalized);


    //We detect whether the player is in the field of view and
write messages in the console accordingly

    if (dotP>minCosine && dotP<=1)

    {

        //in case of detection, the NPC will move towards the
player, following v2, at .5m per seconds

        //Time.deltaTime is the number of seconds since the last
frame

        transform.Translate(v2 * Time.deltaTime*.5f);

        print("player is in sight");

    }

    else

    {

        print("player is out of sight");

    }

}
```

- Then create a new script called **MovePlayer**, and add the script to the player.

```
//The velocity is used to move the NPC forward
Vector3 velocity;
void Start ()
{
    //By default the player is looking in the direction of the
positive z axis
    //we rotate the player around the y axis so that its path
crosses the NPC's field of view
    transform.rotation = Quaternion.Euler(0,-45,0);


    //we set the direction of the player using local coordinates
    velocity = Vector3.forward;
}


void Update ()
{
    //The player will be moving 1 meter forward every second
    //Time.deltaTime corresponds to the number of seconds elapsed
since the last frame
    transform.Translate(velocity * Time.deltaTime*1);

}
```

You can now test your scene:

- Switch to the **Scene** view.

- Move the **player** object so that it enters the **NPC**'s field of view.

- Observe how the **NPC** starts chasing the player.

LEVEL ROUNDUP

Well, this is it!

In this chapter, we have learned about vectors and how they can be used and applied in Unity. We looked at basics properties and operations for vectors, and how these can be combined and employed in games. So, we have, again, covered some significant ground compared to the last chapter, and you should, by now, feel more comfortable using vectors.

Checklist

 You can consider moving to the next chapter if you can do the following:

- Create a vector in Unity.

- Add and subtract vectors.

- Normalize a vector.

- Multiply a vector by a scalar.

Quiz

Now, let's check your knowledge! Please answer the following questions or specify if these statements are either correct or incorrect (the solutions are on the next page).

1. The class **Vector3** can be used to create three-dimensional vectors.

2. The class **Vector2** can be used to create two-dimensional vectors.

3. Unity uses a left-handed coordinate system.

4. A vector can have a direction as well as a length (or magnitude).

5. After normalizing a vector, all its coordinates will be equal to 1.

6. When we multiply a vector by a scalar, the magnitude of the vector remains unchanged.

7. A dot product can be applied to determine the angle between two vectors.

8. The method **Quaternion.Euler** can be used to rotate an object.

9. It is possible to subtract two vectors.

10. In Unity, vectors can be used to simulate forces.

Quiz Solutions

Now, let's check if you have answered the questions correctly.

1. True.

2. False.

3. True.

4. True.

5. True.

6. False.

7. True.

8. True.

9. True.

10. True.

4

COMBINING C# AND UNITY OBJECTS

In this section we will start to look at key C# methods in Unity. You will learn about their syntax, as well as some quick coding recipes to implement some very common game features in Unity. Some of the objectives of this section will be to:

- Understand the C# syntax for Unity.

- Know how to access objects and their component from your scripts.

- Implement useful game mechanics and features through C#.

After completing this chapter, you will be able to:

- Remember the C# syntax when used with Unity.

- Instantiate, activate and destroy objects.

- Find objects and access their components.

- Communicate between scripts.

- Open files (such as XML files) and access other resources from your code.

- Detect objects using collision detection, triggers or ray-casting.

- Access databases through C#.

- Save data across your game.

This chapter effectively acts as a cook book, so you can skip to the subsection of your choice, or read the entire chapter if you wish.

MAPPING OBJECT ORIENTED CONCEPTS TO UNITY

In the previous sections, we have looked at Object-Oriented concepts in order to code in C# and you will be able to implement these specifically for Unity in this chapter.

In Unity, when using C# to create your game, you will be writing statements and creating new classes following an Object-Oriented Programming (OOP) syntax. However, compared to the usual OOP practices, Unity's syntax may seem different, at first glance, even to seasoned developers. So let's try to see how these concepts can be used with Unity.

In Unity most of the objects that you will create in your scene will be instances of the class **GameObject**. The class **GameObject** is therefore the parent (or base class) for any object added to the scene.

Also note that the class **GameObject** provides static functions that can be used without having to instantiate a **GameObject**. For example, the method **GameObject.Find** can help to look for a particular object in your scene.

Any object in the scene can be accessed through your code, based on its name or tag. For example, if we create a new (built-in) **Cube** (i.e., **GameObject | 3D Object | Cube**) called **Cube1** in the **Scene** view, we could access it in our code using the following:

```
GameObject g = GameObject.Find("Cube1");
```

Each **GameObject** has inherited properties such as a transform (to store the position, rotation and scale attributes of the object), a tag, and methods such as **SetActive** (to activate or deactivate the **GameObject**), **AddComponent**, or **GetComponent** to add or access associated components.

So, it is possible to access a **GameObject**'s attributes, components, and methods using the dot notation, as illustrated in the next code snippet.

```
GameObject g;
//g.tag will return the tag
//g.SetActive(false) will deactivate the GameObject.
```

So, so far the notation used to access and modify objects in the scene is quite similar to what we have seen in the previous sections on Object-Oriented Programming.

If you create an object in Unity, a cube for example, you will see, in the **Inspector**, that it also includes **components**. A component usually provides additional features to your object. It can be used to render an object (for example, the **Renderer** component), as a script/class attached to this object (e.g., any new C# class), or to detect collision (for example, the **Collider** component). If you create a new cube primitive in Unity, it will have, by default, the components **Box Collider** and **Mesh Renderer**, along with the attributes **tag**, **layer**, and **Transform**, as illustrated in the next figure.

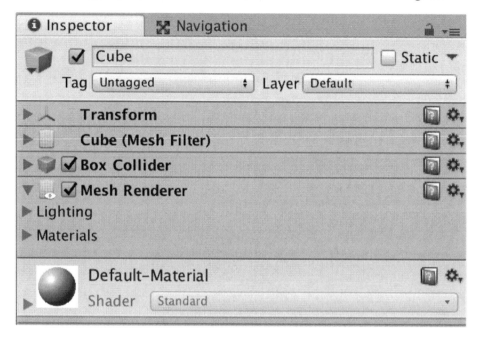

Figure 18: The default components for a cube

To be able to access the components on this object, it is necessary to use member methods. For example, if we wanted to access a new object's **Renderer** component, we could write the following code:

```
Renderer r = g.GetComponent<Renderer>();
```

In the previous code, we specify the type of the component that we want to access by entering its name between the signs "<" (**less than**) and ">" (**greater than**). Similarly, if we wanted to access a component of type **MeshRenderer**, we could have written the following code instead:

```
MeshRenderer r = g.GetComponent<MeshRenderer>();
```

Each component, in turn, is an object that is an instance of a particular class. For example, a **Renderer** can, as for **GameObjects**, include several member methods and variables, and we could decide not to render an object by deactivating its **Renderer** component as follow.

```
Renderer r = g.GetComponent<Renderer>();
r.enabled = false;
```

So again, while a scene includes a collection of **GameObjects**, each **GameObject** includes components that can be accessed and customized through your code.

In addition to being able to access the **GameObjects** in the current scene, Unity also makes it possible to manage scenes through the class **SceneManager**. This class provides utility methods to select, create, load, add, or merge scenes from your code.

The next sections will list and deal with some common sources of confusion when writing C# script in Unity so that you can avoid or solve them quickly.

USING GAMEOBJECT VS. GAMEOBJECT

When you create a C# script in Unity and attach this script to an object, you may need to use either of these keywords; but often, you may wonder which one is correct.

The keyword **gameObject**, when used with a lower case **g**, means the "object linked to this script or the object linked to the current variable". For example, let's look at the following code:

```
void Start ()
{

    float xPos = gameObject.transform.position.x;

}
```

In the previous code:

- We use the **Start** function.

- We record the **x** position for the object linked to the current script.

- To do so, we access the **transform** attribute of the object, then its **position**, and then its **x** coordinate.

The keyword **GameObject**, when used with an upper-case **G**, refers to the class **GameObject**; used this way, it can be employed to declare a new **GameObject** or to access a static method from the class **GameObject**.

Let's look at the first aspect (i.e., new object):

```
GameObject g = new GameObject ();
```

In the previous code, we create a new **GameObject** called **g** and call one of the constructors of the class **GameObject**.

The second aspect is related to static methods which can be accessed without instantiating the class; let's look at the following example:

```
GameObject g2 = GameObject.Find ("Cube1");
```

In the previous code we look for a **GameObject** in the scene called **Cube1**, and we then place the result in the variable **g2**. To so, we employ the static method **GameObject.Find**.

USING GENERIC FUNCTIONS

If you remember the previous sections, we looked into how to access the **Renderer** component of an object called **Cube**, and we could do as follows:

```
MeshRenderer m = GameObject.Find
("Cube1").GetComponent<MeshRenderer>();
```

GetComponent<MeshRenderer>() is usually called a generic function, and you may produce the same code using what is called a non-generic function; however, the former (that is, the generic function) is always more efficient, as it makes your code shorter.

For example, the following code is using a generic function:

```
MeshRenderer m = GameObject.Find
("Cube1").GetComponent<MeshRenderer>();
```

It could, however, have been written with non-generic functions as per the following code:

```
MeshRenderer m2 = (MeshRenderer) GameObject.Find
("Cube").GetComponent(typeof(MeshRenderer));
```

INSTANTIATING AND CASTING

With C#, you will, at some point, need to create (or to instantiate) new **GameObjects**. This can be done in several ways; the first way could be to call the constructor of the class **GameObject** as in the next code.

```
GameObject g = new GameObject ();
```

Another way to instantiate objects is to use the built-in function called **Instantiate**. So, for example, if you wanted to instantiate new bullets based on a prefab (or an existing object), you could use the following code:

```
public GameObject bullet;
void Start ()
{
    GameObject g3 = (GameObject)(Instantiate (bullet,
transform.position, Quaternion.identity));
```

In the previous code:

- We instantiate a new object and save it in the variable **g3**.

- We use the method called **Instantiate** to create a new object; this method takes three parameters: a **GameObject**, a position and a rotation.

Now, the important thing to notice here is that the method **Instantiate** returns a variable of type **Object** and <u>NOT</u> **GameObject**; however, when we create the variable **g3**, we need to make sure that, because the type of the variable **g3** is **GameObject**, that what is returned by the method **Instantiate** is also of type **GameObject**. This is the reason why we use the code "(GameObject)" just before the keyword **Instantiate**: this is called **casting**; using casting, we have converted the type returned by the method **Instantiate** from **Object** to **GameObject**.

You will obviously use casting in other situations; however, when using the **Instantiate** method, this will often be necessary.

Note that casting can also be performed using the keyword **as**, as described in the following code:

```
GameObject g3 = Instantiate (bullet, transform.position,
Quaternion.identity) as GameObject;
```

In the previous code, we use the keywords "**as GameObject**" to specify that the object returned by the method **Instantiate** will be casted as a **GameObject**.

So what is the difference between an Object and a GameObject?

The class **Object** is a base class for all objects that Unity can reference. In other words, any object that is accessible through your code is an instance of an **Object** or inherits from the class **Object**; the **GameObject** class inherits from the class **Object** and refers to objects that can be listed in your scene (i.e., in the **Hierarchy**). This is the reason why the method **Instantiate**, which is a public method for the **Object** class, is also accessible from the class **GameObject**, thanks to inheritance.

Using default methods

When you create a new C# script, Unity will, by default, include two methods to your script; that is: the methods **Start** and **Update**.

- The **Start** method is called whenever the scene (that is, the scene where the object linked to your script is present), is starting. So the **Start** method is usually called once for each of the scenes and this is where you can initialize variables and the content of your scene.

- The **Update** function is called every frame; so it is a good idea to use it sparingly in your code and NOT to include any resource-intensive statements within this method. This being said, there could cases when the **Update** method needs to be used, including for detecting key inputs, for calculating the time (for example, the number of seconds since the last frame was displayed), for working with a **Finite-State Machine**, or for managing the navigation of an NPC.

- In addition to the methods **Start** and **Update**, Unity also provides another method called **Awake**. This method is called at the beginning of the game before the method **Start** is called. It can be used, as we will see later, to initialize objects and to ensure that they are kept throughout the game (across the scenes) using the method **DontDestroyOnLoad**.

CHANGING SCENES, LEVELS, AND MENUS

Game levels and menus are usually organized and structured around scenes. So, to change menu and to go to a specific level, you will usually need to load a new scene. This can be achieved through the class called **SceneManager**, as described in the following code snippet.

```
using System.Collections;
using System.Collections.Generic;
using UnityEngine;
using UnityEngine.SceneManagement;


public class MyScript : MonoBehaviour
{
    public void openNewScene()
    {
        SceneManager.LoadScene ("newScene");
    }
}
```

In the previous code:

- We use the namespace **UnityEngine.SceneManagement**.

- We create a new function where we load a new scene through the static method called **LoadScene**.

- Note that this assumes that: the scene called "**newScene**" has already been created and that it has also been added to the **Build Settings**.

LOOKING FOR OBJECTS

Throughout your game, you will need to find objects included in the scene from your script in order to modify them. To make this easier, Unity provides built-in classes and methods to find an object based on its tag or its name. The following code snippet illustrates some of these methods.

```
GameObject g1 = GameObject.Find ("myCube");

GameObject g2 =
GameObject.FindGameObjectWithTag("onlyAmmmoInScene");

GameObject [] g3 = GameObject.FindGameObjectsWithTag ("ammos");
```

In the previous code:

- We find an object based on its name.

- We find an object based on its tag.

- We find several objects based on their tag. Note that we use an array here because the method **FindObjectsWithTag** returns an array of **GameObjects**.

Because these functions are resource-intensive (that is, Unity may need to go through the full hierarchy of objects to find one or several objects), it is better NOT to use them in the **Update** function.

However, if you want to find an object present in the scene from your script in the **Update** function, you could, as illustrated in the next snippet, find the object in the **Start** function (once), save it in a new variable, and then use this variable in the **Update** function.

```
void Start()
{
    GameObject g1 = GameObject.Find ("myCube");
}
void Update()
{
    g1.SetActive(false);
}
```

COMMUNICATING BETWEEN SCRIPTS

In your game, most of your scripts will generally be linked to an object. Because these scripts include different types of information, you may sometimes need these scripts to communicate between each other. So. let's say that you have two different scripts **Script1** and **Script2**, each linked to the objects **Object1** and **Object2**, respectively.

- The content of **Script2** could be as follows:

```
public class Script2 : MonoBehaviour
{
    private string firstName;
    void Start()
    {
        firstName = "John";
    }
    public  string getFName()
    {
        return (firstName);
    }
}
```

In the previous code:

- We declare a string variable called **firstName** and it is private, so it will only be accessible from instances of the class **Script2**.

- We initialize the variable **firstName** in the method **Start**.

- We then declare a method called **getFName** that returns the value of the member variable **firstName**; note that this method is public and it will therefore be accessible throughout our game.

We could create a new script called **Script1** that will access the other script **Script2**.

The content of **Script1** could be as follows:

```
void Start ()
{
      string nameFromTheOtherScript = GameObject.Find
("Object2").GetComponent<Script2> ().getFName ();
      print ("name is " + nameFromTheOtherScript);
}
void Update () {}
```

In the previous code:

- We create a new string variable called **nameFromTheOtherScript**.

- We access the method called **getFName** from the script **Script2**, that is a component of the object called **Object2**.

- We then save the value returned by the method **getFName** in the variable called **nameFromTheOtherScript**.

So, based on the previous steps, we just need to remember that:

- A script, when attached to an object, is seen as a component; it can, therefore, once we have identified the corresponding object, be accessed using the method **GetComponent**.

- If methods or variables that belong to this script are public, they should then be accessible from outside the script.

- Using this approach, we could access attributes of any of the components (including scripts) linked to a particular objet.

GENERATING RANDOM NUMBERS AND LOCATIONS

In your games, there are several cases when you will need Mathematics for generating random numbers, performing a conversion between units or using the modulo operator; so let's look at each of these aspects.

First let's look at random numbers.

Random numbers can be used in many cases including when you want to choose a random path for an NPC, add objects at a random location in your game, or open a random scene. In all these cases, you may need to generate a random number.

Luckily, Unity provides a static function called **Random.Range** that returns a float variable that is a random number between (and inclusive of) the lower and upper boundary of a range that you can define, as illustrated in the next example.

```
float randomFloat = Random.Range (0.0f, 12.0f);

print ("Random Float:" + randomFloat);

int randomNumber = Random.Range (0, 3);

//using an int variable means that the upper boundary is excluded


Vector3 [] randomPosition = new Vector3 [3] { new Vector3(0,0,0),
new Vector3(1,1,1), new Vector3(3,2,3)};

Vector3 newPosition = randomPosition [randomNumber];

print ("Random Position:" + newPosition);
```

In the previous code:

- We create and display a random number as a float. Because we ask to generate a float variable, the number will range between the lower and the upper boundary and include both the lower and the upper boundary.

- We then create and display a random number as an integer; because we ask to generate an int variable, the number will range between the lower and the upper boundary, excluding the upper boundary.

- In the next part of the snippet, we are generating code that will select a random location, where we could, for example, instantiate objects. The random location is selected amongst different values from an array of positions (which are vectors). We then select one of these vectors based on the random number selected earlier.

USING THE MODULO OPERATOR

Now, let's look at the **modulo** operator.

It is quite common to use additions, subtractions, multiplications or divisions to be able to, for example, calculate a score, a bonus, or penalty points. However, there are also interesting situations where the modulo operator can be used.

Put simply, the **modulo** provides the remainder of a division. When designing games, this can be used very efficiently in several cases, including: when you want to organize the content of a simple array into a two- or three-dimensional space, or to, for example, create a timer and find minutes and hours based on the number of seconds elapsed.

Let's look at the next snippet to see how the modulo operator can be used to map the content of an array to 3D coordinates.

```
void Start()
{
    int [] myArray = new int[25]
    {
        1,1,1,1,1,1,1,1,1,1,1,1,1,1,1,1,1,1,1,1,1,1,1,1,1
    };
    for (int i=0; i <= myArray.Length-1; i++)
    {
        GameObject g = GameObject.CreatePrimitive
(PrimitiveType.Sphere);
        if (myArray[i]==1) Instantiate (g, new Vector3(i % 5,
0, i / 5), Quaternion.identity);
    }
}
```

In the previous code:

- We create an array of 25 integers.

- We then go through the array using a loop.

- If the current item in the array includes the number 1 then we instantiate a new **Sphere** primitive accordingly.

- The position of the sphere is based on the variable **i**, using the division and the modulo operators to specify the **x** and **z** coordinates of the new object.

- By using **i/5** and **i%5** we effectively manage to subdivide the array into chunks of 5 sets (or rows), and this can be illustrated as follows:

```
int [] myArray = new int[25]
{
    1,1,1,1,1,
    1,1,1,1,1,
    1,1,1,1,1,
    1,1,1,1,1,
    1,1,1,1,1
};
```

In the previous code, the array has been presented differently to show that it could be broken down into 5 rows with 5 items (or numbers) each.

If you were to link the previous code to an empty object in Unity, you would obtain a scene that may look like the next figure.

Figure 19: Using the modulo operator to create a scene

CONVERSION BETWEEN DEGREES AND RADIANS

When you are using angles in Unity, it may sometimes be necessary to perform conversions between radians and degrees or vice versa. To achieve this purpose, you can use the methods **MathfRad2Deg** or **MathfDeg2Rad**. There is no reason to use degrees more than radians, but this choice will essentially depend on the type of the argument required for the methods that you are using. Degrees range from 0 to 360 whereas radians range from 0 to 2*PI. For example, when you need to calculate the **Sine** of an angle, the method **Mathf.Sin** calculates the **Sine** of an angle expressed in radians; so if your angle is initially expressed in degrees, it will need to be converted using the method **MathfDeg2Rad**.

CREATING A TIMER AND PAUSING THE GAME

In most of the games that you will create, you will, more than likely, include the concept of time. This may mean a timer indicating how much time remains before the player loses, or simply, the ability to pause the game.

Implementing a Timer

So first, let's look at the following snippet example that implements a timer:

```
float time;
void Update()
{
    time += Time.deltaTime;
    float seconds, minutes, hours;
    seconds = time % 60;
    minutes = time / 60;
    hours = time / 3600;
    print ((int)hours + ":" + (int)minutes + ":" +
(int)seconds);
}
```

In the previous code:

- We use the **Update** function.

- We calculate the time since the game started and save it in the variable called time.

- We then calculate the current seconds, minutes, and hours based on the variable time.

If you were to create a countdown, the principle would remain the same, except that the variable **time** would be initialized to a value that is greater than zero and then decreased every seconds until it reaches zero.

Pausing the Game

In Unity, it is very simple to pause or resume your game, using the following code:

```
Time.timeScale = 0;//time is paused
Time.timeScale = 1;//time is back to normal
```

So, you could for example, create two buttons and functions: one button (and its associated function) for pausing the game as well as one button (and its associated function) for resuming the game. You could then call one of these functions based on the button that the player has pressed.

CREATING, ACTIVATING OR DESTROYING OBJECTS

As we have seen previously, it is possible to instantiate objects using the **Instantiate** function; and it is also possible to destroy or to deactivate an object accordingly.

You can use the method called **Destroy** to destroy an object either instantaneously or after a specific delay, as illustrated in the next code snippet.

```
void Start ()
{

    Destroy (gameObject, 5);

    Destroy (GameObject.Find ("Cube"));

}
```

In the previous code:

- We use the function **Start**.

- We destroy the object linked to this script after a delay of 5 seconds. This could be used for bullets or any object that would typically disappear a few seconds after its creation. Note that we use **gameObject** with a lowercase **g** as we refer to the object linked to this particular script.

- In the second line, we look for an object called **Cube** and we destroy it instantaneously.

There are also times where it is good not to destroy an object, but instead, to deactivate it; for example, you may want an object to appear in the scene only after the player has collected some items. This can be useful for treasure hunts, or adventure games based on exploration. In this case you would typically do the following:

- Add the object to the scene manually. While you could do this through code, doing this manually has the advantage, especially for bulky objects, to know exactly where and how the object will fit in the scene. Of course, if you had to do this for several objects, a script-based instantiation may be more efficient.

- Make sure that the object is activated in the **Scene** by checking the **Inspector**.

- Create a reference to the object in your script before it is deactivated.

- Deactivate the object from your script at the start of the scene.

- Reactivate the object from your script when an event has occurred (for example, when the player has collected all relevant items).

This could be implemented using the following code:

```
public class DestroyAndDeactivate : MonoBehaviour {
GameObject g;
bool collectedItems;
void Start ()
{
      g = GameObject.Find ("Cube2");
      g.SetActive (false);
}
void Update ()
{
      if (collectedItems && !g.activeInHierarchy) g.SetActive
(true);
}
```

In the previous code:

- We declare the variable **g** that will be used as a reference to the object that we need to hide or deactivate.

- We also declare a **Boolean** variable that will be used to know whether the necessary items to activate the object have been collected.

- Then, in the function **Start**, we find the object called **Cube2** and we link it to the variable **g**.

- Through the variable **g**, we deactivate the object **Cube2**.

- In the **Update** function, we then check that the object **Cube2** is no longer active. We also check that the items have been collected and if this is the case, we then activate the object **Cube2**.

So this approach is very useful when you want to show some items based on conditions; and you can also, as we have seen earlier, destroy these objects either instantaneously or after a delay.

This being said, there are cases when you may want to make sure objects (and any related component or children) are not destroyed when transitioning between scenes. You see, when you load a new scene, by default all the objects in the previous scene are destroyed before the objects from the new scene are instantiated. So, there are cases when you don't want this to happen; for example, if you have a game manager object that should be kept across scenes.

In this case, you could use the following snippet and attach the corresponding script to the object that you'd like to keep between scenes.

```
void Awake()
{
    DontDestroyOnLoad(transform.gameObject);
}
```

In the previous code:

- We implement the method called **Awake** that is usually called when the script is loaded; this method is called only once in the lifetime of the game.

- We then use the method **DontDestroyOnLoad** to ask Unity to keep this particular object and its children.

- The method **Start** is not used in this case, as it is often called every time a scene is starting; however, in our case, we just want to execute this code once in the game, and the method **Awake** is therefore more relevant for this purpose.

TRANSFORMING, FOLLOWING, AND ACCESSING OBJECTS

As we have seen earlier, whenever an object is created in the **Scene** view, it includes a **Transform** attribute that includes information about the object's position, rotation and scale. So Unity provides several useful functions to modify these parameters so that you can translate, rotate, or scale an object from a script. Let's look at the following snippet to see how it can be done:

```
void Start ()
{

    GameObject g = GameObject.Find ("Cube");

    g.transform.Translate(new Vector3(1,0,0));

    g.transform.Rotate (new Vector3 (0, 45, 0));

    g.transform.localScale = new Vector3(2, 2, 2);

}
```

In the previous code:

- We create a reference to the object called **Cube**.

- We then move this object to a new position.

- We also rotate this object using the function **Rotate**. The rotation uses **Euler Angle**s. So we use a vector notation to perform the rotation: the x coordinate indicates the amount of rotation (in degrees) around the x axis, the y coordinate indicates the amount of rotation (in degrees) around the y axis, and the z coordinate indicates the amount of rotation (in degrees) around the z axis. So in our case, we rotate the object 45 degrees around its y axis.

- In the last line of code, we rescale the object, using a vector notation for which the x, y and z coordinates indicate the scale factor on the x-, y- and z-axes, respectively.

Now there are times when you'd like to perform a smooth transformation overtime for an object. In this particular case, you can use a **Lerp** (that is, a linear interpolation). In Unity, a Lerp will be used to perform an interpolation between two values (two vectors, two colors, or two angles).

Interpolating means that given two values (that is, an initial and an ending value), we can compute the values in-between. Let's take the example of a journey between two cities A and B. If we progress at a constant speed, and we know our starting time and the time of arrival (or the duration of the journey), we can predict at what time we will have completed half of the journey: this is called **interpolation**. So let's look at how this could be applied to a **translation** in Unity with the following code.

```
GameObject g;

float startTime, currentTime, duration;

void Start ()

{

    g = GameObject.Find ("Cube");

    startTime = Time.time;

    duration = 5;

}

void Update ()

{

    currentTime = Time.time;

    float percentage = (currentTime - startTime) / (duration);

    g.transform.position = Vector3.Lerp (new Vector3 (1, 0, 0),
new Vector3 (10, 0, 0), percentage);

}
```

In the previous code:

- We declare the variable **g**, as we have done before.

- We also declare three variables called: **startTime**, **currentTime** and **duration**.

- The variables **startTime** and **duration** are initialized in the **Start** function.

- At this stage, we have set the variables to be used for the **Lerp**; however, when using a Lerp, we need to specify the initial position, the end position, as well as the percentage of progression between the starting and ending states. In other words, we need to be able to determine the proportion of the journey that we have completed so far.

- This can be done by establishing a number that ranges from 0 to 1 (i.e., 0 means not completed and 1 means fully completed) and that can be calculated as a ratio between the time elapsed since the start of the journey (i.e., **currentTime - startTime**) and the full duration of the journey (i.e., the variable **duration**).

- So the last line completes this tasks by using the method **Vector3.Lerp** and by specifying the start position **(1, 0, 0)**, the end position **(10, 0, 0)** as well as the percentage of the journey that has been completed at this stage (i.e., a percentage).

This technique is very useful and you can, of course, apply the same principle to perform interpolations between floats (using **Mathf.Lerp**), rotational values saved as Quaternions (using **Quaternion.Lerp**) or colors (using **Color.Lerp**).

In addition to moving objects, the **Transform** class also offers some other interesting features such as searching for an object's children. This can be done using the method **Transform.Find**, as illustrated in the next code snippet.

Let's imagine that we have created an object called **Cube1** and that we have also created two other objects called **Cube2** and **Cube3** that are children of the object **Cube1.** This could be achieved, for example by dragging and dropping these two objects **Cube2** and **Cube3** on the object **Cube1** in the **Hierarchy**) as illustrated in the next figure.

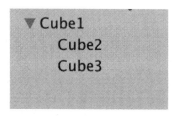

Figure 20: Creating a hierarchy of objects

So we could create a script that is linked to the parent object (i.e., **Cube1**) and that finds some of the children of the object called **Cube1**, as follows:

```
void Start ()
{

    Transform t2 = transform.Find ("Cube2");

    Transform t3 = transform.GetChild (0);

    print (t2.gameObject.name+" was found as a child of "
+gameObject.name);

    print (t3.gameObject.name+" is the first child of "+
gameObject.name);

}
```

In the previous code:

- We declare two **Transform** objects **t2** and **t3**. This is because the functions **transform.Find** and **transform.GetChild** both return a **Transform** object.

- **t2** refers to the transform attribute of the object **Cube2**.

- **t3** refers to the transform attribute of the first child of the current object; note that the child at the index **0** is the first child. In the scene, the first child of an object is the child that is the highest in the **Hierarchy** or the closest to the parent.

- We then print information about these two objects. The name of the GameObject linked to **t2** is retrieved using the syntax: **t2.gameObject**. We use a lower case for the word **gameObject** here as we refer to the object – not the class – that is linked to the transform.

- The same is performed with **t3**.

The method **GetChild** is useful when you just want to access an item that is the child of a specific object. For example, if all NPCs in your scene have a **gun** with a label called **gun**, and you want to deactivate the **gun** of a specific NPC, then the method **GetChild** might be handy. If you were to use **GameObject.FindWithTag("gun")**, this method would return all the guns with a tag called **gun** in the scene. However, if, instead, you select a particular NPC, the object that corresponds to its gun, and named **gun**, can be found using the syntax **npc.getChild("gun")**, provided that the gun is a child of the NPC.

Last but not least, we will look at the method called **LookAt**. This method is useful when you would like a character or an object to face a particular direction. This can be used for NPCs to make sure that they always look at the player. This could also be used so that a camera is always looking at a particular item in your scene. Let's look at how this can be done using the following snippet.

```
void Update ()
{
    transform.LookAt (GameObject.Find ("target").transform);
}
```

In the previous code:

- We use the **Update** function so that the information is updated frequently, because the object that we are looking at may move over time.

- We then use the method **LookAt** to make sure that the current object is oriented towards an object called **target**.

- Because the method **LookAt** works with **Transforms**, we need to obtain the transform from the object that we want to look at.

USING VECTORS FOR DISTANCE AND POSITION

When adding or moving objects in the **Scene**, you will probably use the classes **Vector3** or **Vector2**. These classes can be used to create two-dimensional or three-dimensional vectors. In addition, the classes **Vector2** and **Vector3** provide static methods to calculate the distance between two positions (for example between two objects) or to easily move objects in different directions (for example, left, right, forward, back, up, or down).

First let's look at how you would calculate the distance between two objects. This could be used, for example, to determine how far you are from a specific NPC, to check if it can hear you.

```
void Update ()
{

    float distance =
Vector3.Distance(gameObject.transform.transform.position,
GameObject.Find("target").transform.position);

    print("distance");

}
```

In the previous code:

- We declare a float variable called **distance** that will be used to calculate the distance between the current object (i.e., the object linked to this script) and the object called **target**.

- We then use the static method **Vector3.Distance**; it takes two parameters: the position of the first object and the position of the second object.

- We then print the value of the variable **distance**.

To be able to move an object to the right or to the left, or in any other direction, we could use the following code.

```
void Start ()
{
     GameObject.Find ("target").transform.position +=
Vector3.right;
}
```

Note that: **Vector3.right** is equivalent to the vector **(1, 0, 0)**; so the previous code would add the vector **(1, 0, 0)** to the current position; however, there may be cases when you want this object to be moved to the right in relation to its own position; in this case, you could use the following code instead.

```
Transform g = GameObject.Find ("target").transform;
g.position += g.right;
```

In the previous code, the object will be moved to its right.

Similarly, the vectors **Vector3.up** and **Vector3.down** correspond to the vector **(0, 1, 0)** and **(0, -1, 0)** and can be used to move an object slightly up or down.

All these vectors (i.e., **Vector3.right**, **Vector3.left**, etc.) are **unit** vectors or **normalized** vectors which means that their length or magnitude is 1. So, if you would like objects to be moved up by two meters (instead of one) you can multiply these vectors by a scalar, as illustrated in the next snippet.

```
Transform g = GameObject.Find ("target").transform;
g.position += 2*g.right;
```

MANAGING USER INPUTS (KEYSTROKES)

In many of the games that you will develop, you will need to add interaction and means for the player to control characters or to enter information. This can be done in different ways, including: key strokes (for example when keys are pressed or released), mouse movements (for example when the mouse is over an area or when it is being dragged and dropped), game controllers, or touch (for tablets and smart phones). So in the next paragraphs and sections we will look at how user inputs can be detected.

Keystrokes can be detected using the methods **Input.GetKey**, **Input.GetKeyDown**, or **Input.GetKeyUp**. The former tests whether a key is currently being pressed while the other two test whether a key has just been pressed or released. In all cases, we will be looking for a specific key code that refers to the key that has been pressed or released on the keyboard.

The following code provides an example of how these three methods can be used.

```
void Update ()
{

    if (Input.GetKey (KeyCode.A)) print ("The key A is being
pressed");

    if (Input.GetKeyDown (KeyCode.A)) print ("The key A has been
pressed");

    if (Input.GetKeyUp (KeyCode.A)) print ("The key A has been
released");

}
```

If you use the previous code and press and release the key **A** on your keyboard, the first message may be displayed several times (as it is checked every frame), whereas the last two messages will be displayed only once because they are called only when the player either starts or stops to press a key.

To have a full list of the key codes to be used with these methods, you can check the official documentation (https://docs.unity3d.com/ScriptReference/KeyCode.html). Note that in addition to keyboard keys, these functions also make it possible to detect mouse clicks and also when joysticks buttons are pressed.

To save you some code (and time), if you wanted to check (and write the corresponding code) for all the letters on the keyboard, instead of writing 24 conditional statements to check for the 24 possible keys pressed, you could instead use a slightly different way of detecting the key pressed by the player. This method will involve checking if a key has been pressed and then checking if this key is a letter.

The code could look as follows:

```
void checkKeyboard2()
{
    if (Input.anyKeyDown)
    {
        char letterPressed = Input.inputString.ToCharArray ()
[0];
        int letterPressedAsInt = System.Convert.ToInt32
(letterPressed);
        if (letterPressedAsInt >= 97 && letterPressed <= 122)
        {
            for (int i=0; i < lengthOfWordToGuess; i++)
            {
                if (!lettersGuessed [i])
                {
    letterPressed = System.Char.ToUpper (letterPressed);
                    if (lettersToGuess [i] ==
letterPressed)
                    {
                        lettersGuessed [i] = true;

    GameObject.Find("letter"+(i+1)).GetComponent<Text>().text =
letterPressed.ToString();
                    }
                }
            }
        }
    }
}
```

In the previous code:

- We detect whether a key has been pressed using the method **Input.anyKeyDown**.

- If a key has been pressed, we save the key (i.e., the letter) that was pressed into the variable called **letterPressed**. Given that any key pressed on the keyboard is stored as a string, we need to convert this string value to a character; the character recorded in the variable **letterPressed** will effectively be the first character of the string that corresponds to the key pressed by the player.

- Once this is done, we convert the letter pressed (i.e., character) to an integer value.

- We then check, using the integer value associated with the key pressed (that is **letterPressedAsInt**), that the key is a letter, which means that the variable **letterPressedAsInt** should be between **97** and **122**.

DETECTING USER INPUTS (MOUSE MOVEMENTS)

In Unity, mouse movements in relation to other objects can be detected and processed by specific methods, for example:

- **OnMouseDown**: this method is used to detect when the player has pressed the left button of the mouse while the mouse is over an object that includes a collider.

- **OnMouseEnter**: this method is used to detect when the player has moved the mouse over an object that includes a collider.

- **OnMouseExit**: this method is used to detect when the player has moved away from an object that includes a collider.

For example, to detect mouse movements over a sprite in Unity, you could create a sprite with a **2D Collider** component, and attach a script with the following code to it.

```
void OnMouseOver()
{
    print ("Mouse is over");
}
void OnMouseEnter()
{
    print ("Just Entered the zone defined by the Sprite");
}
void OnMouseExit()
{
    print ("Just Exited the zone defined by the Sprite");
}
```

In the previous code, we implement three methods that process specific mouse events.

MANAGING USER INPUTS (DRAG AND DROP)

When designing your game, you may want to detect when the user clicks on an object (such as a sprite) or when s/he drags this object across the screen. So, in the next steps we will see how to implement the **drag** function, which is the ability for the player to drag an object across the screen. For this, we will simply make sure that, once the player drags the mouse over an object, the position of the object is the same as the position of the mouse.

So we will create a function that will be called every time an object is dragged (that is, after the player performs a left click and then moves the mouse), and that will update the position of the object accordingly, so that it is at the same position as the mouse over time, hence creating a dragging movement.

So, to create this effect, you could follow the next steps:

- Create a sprite (that is, an image) that we will be able to drag and drop.

- Create a new **Image** (by selecting **GameObject | UI | Image**) and rename it **image**.

- This will create a white square, as illustrated in the next figure.

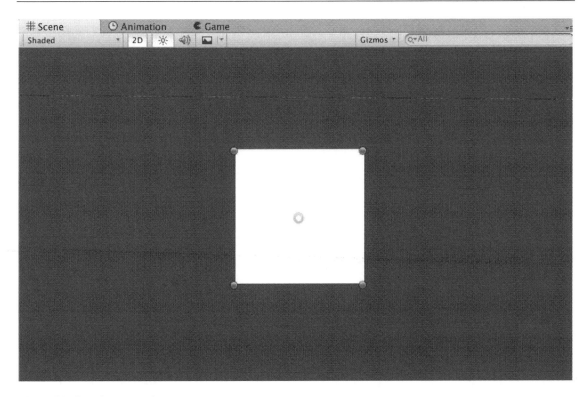

Figure 21: Creating a new image

- Create a new script called **DragAndDrop** (i.e., from the **Project** menu, select: **Create | C# Script**).

- Open this script (i.e., double click on the script **DragAndDrop** in the **Project** window).

- Add the following code to it (just before the end of the class).

```
public void Drag ()
{
    GameObject.Find("image").transform.position =
Input.mousePosition;

    print("Dragging" + gameObject.name);
}
```

In the previous code, the position of the object called **image** will be the same as the position of the mouse. This function will be called when the object is dragged.

- Save this script, and add it (i.e., drag and drop it) to the object **image**.

- Select the object called **image** from the **Hierarchy**.

- Using the **Inspector**, add a component called **Event Trigger** (**Component | Event | Event Trigger**) to the object **image**.

- The following new component should now appear in the **Inspector** for the object image.

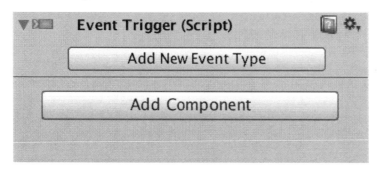

Figure 22: Adding an Event Trigger component (part 1)

- In the component **Event Trigger**, click on the button called **Add New Event Type** (as illustrated in the next figure) and then choose the option called **Drag** from the drop-down menu.

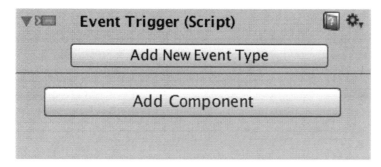

Figure 23: Adding an Event Trigger component (part 2)

- A new field called **Drag (BaseEventData)** should appear, as illustrated in the next figure.

- Click on the + sign that is below the label **List is Empty**, as illustrated in the next figure.

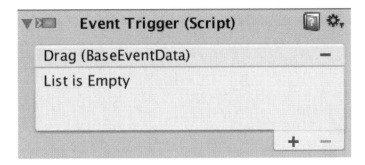

Figure 24: Configuring the new event (part1)

- This will create a new empty field with the label **None (Object)**.

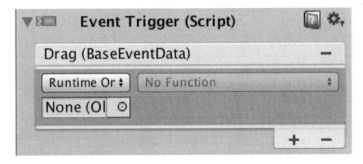

Figure 25:Configuring the new event (part 2)

- Drag and drop the object called **image** from the **Hierarchy** window to this field.

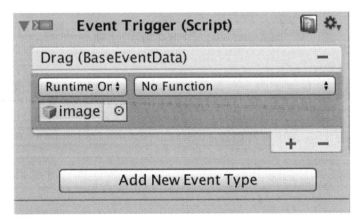

Figure 26: Configuring the new event (part 3)

- Next, you can click on the drop-down menu entitled **No Function**, and select the option **DragAndDrop | Drag**, as illustrated in the next figure.

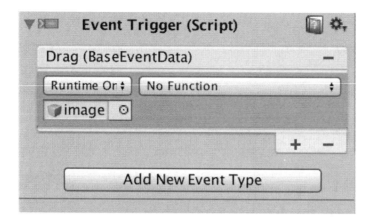

Figure 27: Configuring the new event (part 4)

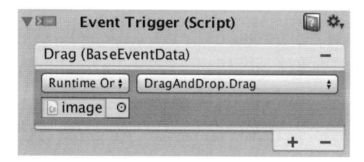

Figure 28: Configuring the new event (part 5)

You can now test your scene, and you should be able to drag the white square around the screen.

Now that we can drag and drop the image, we can add a placeholder and modify our code so that the image snaps to the placeholder if it is dropped close enough.

So the process will consist in:

- Creating a new image for the placeholder.

- Dropping the image near the placeholder.

- Checking the distance between the placeholder and the image.

- Placing the image atop the placeholder if the image is close enough.

- Placing the image back to its original position otherwise.

So let's proceed:

- Please create a new image (**Game Object | UI | Image**).

- Rename this image **PH1** (as in **P**lace**H**older **1**).

- Move this object **PH1** to the right of the object called **image**.

- Change the color of the object **PH1** to green, using the **Inspector**.

Figure 29: Adding a placeholder

Now that the placeholder (i.e., green square) has been created, we will create a new function in the script called **DragAndDrop**, that will be called when the user drops the image.

- Please open the script **DragAndDrop**.

- Add the following function at the end of the class.

```
public void Drop()
{
    GameObject ph1 = GameObject.Find("PH1");

    GameObject img = GameObject.Find("image");

    float distance = Vector3.Distance(ph1.transform.position,
img.transform.position);

    if (distance <= 50)
    {
        img.transform.position = ph1.transform.position;
    }
}
```

In the previous code:

- We create two **GameObjects** that refer to the objects **image** and **PH1** that we have created earlier.

- We calculate the distance between the object called **image** and the object **PH1** (that is, the placeholder).

- If this distance is less than 50, then the object called **image** is moved to the same position as the placeholder; this is the "snapping" effect that was mentioned earlier.

- Please save your code and check that it is error-free.

Now, we just need to add a new event to the object **image** to detect when the player drops (or stops dragging) the image; we will then link this event to the new function that we have just created (i.e., **Drop**).

- Please select the object called **image** in the **Hierarchy**.

- Using the **Inspector**, in the component called **Event Trigger**, click on the button called **Add New Event Type**.

Figure 30: Creating a new event (part 1)

- From the drop-down menu select the event called **End Drag**; this will create a new event, as illustrated on the next figure.

Figure 31: Creating a new event (part 2)

- Once this done, click on the drop-down menu to the right of the label **Runtime**, as illustrated in the next figure.

Figure 32: Creating a new event (part 2)

- From the drop-down menu, select: **DragAndDrop | Drop**, to indicate that, in case the player stops dragging the image, then the function called **Drop** should be called.

Figure 33: Creating a new event (part 3)

- Using the **Hierarchy**, you can also move (i.e., drag and drop) the object called **image** so that it is the second element listed within the object **Canvas**, as illustrated in the next figure; this is so that it is displayed atop the placeholder when dragged and dropped.

Figure 34: Moving the object image down the Hierarchy

You can now test your scene, and you should see that, as you drag and drop the image close to the placeholder, the image snaps to the placeholder.

MANAGING USER INPUTS FOR MOBILE DEVICES (I.E., TAPS)

If you create a mobile game, you will need to detect the players' taps onscreen. While detecting interaction with buttons remains the same on mobile devices, taps are rather different in that you need to use a different method called **Input.touchCount** that will detect how many times the player's fingers have touched the screen simultaneously. Note that Unity also makes it possible to detect where exactly the player has touched the screen.

So, you could create an empty object and add the following code to the **Update** function as follows.

```
if (Input.touchCount > 0)
{
    Touch touch = Input.GetTouch (0);
    if (touch.position.x > Screen.width / 2) jump ();
}
```

In the previous code:

- We detect whether the player has touched the screen.

- When it was detected that one (or several) fingers has touched the screen, it is possible to obtain more information using the method **Input.GetTouch**. This method returns a **Touch** object that correspond to each of the fingers that have touched the screen. The index used when calling the function **Input.GetTouch**, starts with the first finger to touch the screen. So if you touched the screen with two fingers, **Input.GetTouch(0)** will return information about the first finger that touched the screen, and **Input.getTouch(1)** will return information about the second finger that touched the screen, and so on. Using an index number that is greater than **1** is essentially applicable to devices that support **multi-touch**.

- Wet then check whether the player has tapped on the right side of the screen, and we call the **jump** function if this is the case. This is done by determining the screen size using the syntax **Screen.width**.

USING THE ARROW KEYS FOR MOVEMENT

In Unity, you can use the arrow keys (or, alternatively, the keys W, A, S and D) to move objects using the method called **Input.GetAxis**. This method maps these keys to a specific axis. For example, we could map the **left** and **right** arrows as opposing directions along the x axis (which is often referred as the **horizontal** axis) and the **up** and **down** arrows as opposing directions along the y axis (which is often referred as the **vertical** axis). We could then use this mapping to move an object with the arrow keys along the axes defined earlier, as illustrated in the next code example.

```
void Update ()
{

    float xMove = Input.GetAxis ("Horizontal");

    float yMove = Input.GetAxis ("Vertical");

    transform.Translate (xMove, yMove, 0);

}
```

In the previous code:

- In Unity, an **Axis** object can either be **Horizontal** or **Vertical**.

- We map the float variable **xMove** to the **Horizontal** axis. This means that the arrow keys (or the keys **A** and **D**) will correspond to opposite directions (+1 and -1) along this axis.

- We map the float variable to the **Vertical** axis. This means that the arrow keys (or the keys **W** and **S**) will correspond to opposite directions (+1 and -1) along this axis.

- We then translate the object linked to this script, along the corresponding axis, and this is done every frame. So if you press the left arrow, the object should start to move to the left.

PLAYING AUDIO

It is always a good idea to provide feedback to users in your games, and this feedback can be provided in many forms, including audio. Audio can also be employed for background music.

In Unity, background audio and special sound effects can be implemented using **Audio Source** components and **Audio Clips**.

An **Audio Source** can be compared to a sound system (or an MP3 player) with a charger for different CDs or tracks, whereas an **Audio Clip** can be compared to the actual track to be played.

Whether you want to include a background music or a sound effect in your game, the procedure will probably be similar to the following:

- Add (or use the existing) **Audio Source** component to/from an object.

- Import an audio file into Unity.

- Select this audio file as the "tune" (i.e., the **AudioClip**) to be played by the sound system (i.e., the **AudioSource**).

- Play the sound whenever it is required.

So you would usually do as follows:

- Add an **AudioSource** component to an object.

- Create a new script and link it to the same object.

- Add the following code to the beginning of the script.

```
AudioClip pickupSound;
```

- This code creates a placeholder for the **Audio Clip** that we want to play.

- Using the **Project** window, drag and drop the audio clip that you have imported to the **pickupSound** placeholder that appears for the script attached to your object in the **Inspector**.

- Add the following code to your script where you want to play the sound that you have imported.

```
gameObject.GetComponent.<AudioSource>().clip= pickupSound;
gameObject.GetComponent.<AudioSource>().Play();
```

In the previous code:

- We access the **Audio Source** component of the object linked to this script.

- We mention that the current clip to be played is **pickupSound**, and we then play the current clip.

- Note that if you wanted to play multiple sounds, you would just need to add another public **AudioClip** variable to the script, to drag and drop another clip to the script using the **Inspector**, and to play it accordingly.

WORKING WITH RIGIDBODY COMPONENTS

As you may already know, **Rigidbody** components make it possible to apply physics behaviors to objects, so that they can be subject to forces such as gravity. These components can be useful when simulating projectiles.

For example, we could create and apply a force to a projectile in your game. To do so, we can use a method that is available for all rigid bodies, called **AddForce**. This method adds a force to a specific **Rigidbody** component, based on a direction and a magnitude (or intensity), as illustrated in the next code snippet.

```
gameObject.GetComponent<Rigidbody>().AddForce(transform.forward *
500);
```

In the previous code, we access the **Rigidbody** component of our object and we then add a force forward with an intensity of **500**.

We could of course apply the same principle to a 2D game to implement a shooter for example as follows.

- Add the following code at the beginning of the script (new code in bold).

```
public class MovePlayer : MonoBehaviour
{

    public GameObject bullet;
```

- Add the following code to the **Update** function:

```
if (Input.GetKeyDown (KeyCode.Space))
{

    GameObject b = (GameObject)(Instantiate (bullet,
transform.position + transform.up*1.5f, Quaternion.identity));

    b.GetComponent<Rigidbody2D> ().AddForce (transform.up *
1000);
}
```

In the previous code:

- We create a new **GameObject**.

- This **GameObject** will be based on the template called **bullet**.

- If the player hits the space bar, a new bullet will be instantiated just above the spaceship.

- We then add an upward force to the bullet so that it starts to move.

DETECTING OBJECTS WITH TRIGGERS AND COLLIDERS

In your games, you will often need to detect collisions between objects. This can be related to NPCs or objects that you will collect or interact with. For this purpose, you can use (and monitor) colliders. However, the way you manage collisions, and the methods to be called in this case, will highly depend on the type of colliders used (for example, colliders or triggers) as well as the object from which you want to detect the collision (for example, simple objects or character controllers).

So, let's start with the most likely scenario where you have to collect objects using a first-person controller. You could create a script, add the following code to it, and drag and drop the script on the **FPSController** object.

```
void OnControllerColliderHit(ControllerColliderHit hit)
{
    print ("Collisding with" + hit.collider.gameObject.name);
}
```

In the previous code, we detect collision between the player (when it is in in movement) and other colliders in the scene. This method returns a **ControllerColliderHit** object that provides information about the collision, including the collider involved and its associated **GameObject**.

Next, we could try to detect collision between a third-person controller and other objects. So you could create a script, add the following code to it, and drag and drop the script on the **ThirdPersonController** object. This code will work because the methods **OnCollisionEnter** and **OnCollisionExit** require a collision between a rigid body and a collider and since the **ThirdPersonController** object includes a rigid body then these conditions are fulfilled.

```
void OnCollisionEnter(Collision c)
{
print ("Player collided with" + c.collider.gameObject.name);
}


void OnCollisionExit(Collision c)
{
print ("Player stopped colliding with" +
c.collider.gameObject.name);


}
```

In the previous code, we use both the methods **OnCollisionEnter** and **OnCollisionExit**, and, each time, we display the name of the object that is (or was) colliding with the character.

In addition to the two previous examples, when you want to detect collision between your character and other objects, you might also want to detect when your character is entering a specific zone. For example, it may be the case that an alarm should be raised when the player enters a specific room, or maybe the player's energy should replenish after entering a "healthy" area. In both cases, you don't need to detect collisions. Instead, you just need to define an area based on a spherical, cylindrical or cubical primitive and call a specific function when an object enters this area.

To define areas that act as triggers, you can use simple primitives (for example a cube, a sphere or a cylinder). When you create a primitive in Unity, it will include a collider by default, and this collider can be set to a normal mode (that is, the **collider** mode) or to a **trigger** mode. This can be done using the **Inspector**, as illustrated in the next figure, by enabling or disabling the attribute called **IsTrigger**.

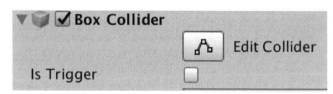

Figure 35: Using triggers

In our case, we would need to:

- Set the parameter **IsTriger** to **true**.

- Deactivate the **Renderer** for this box so that the trigger area is not visible in the game.

- Add the following code to a script attached to either a **First-** or a **Third-Person Controller** as follows.

```
void OnTriggerEnter (Collider otherObject)
{
     print ("Just entered the trigger defined by the object " +
otherObject.gameObject.name);
}


void OnTriggerExit (Collider otherObject)
{
     print ("Just exited the trigger defined by the object " +
otherObject.gameObject.name);
}
```

In the previous code, we use both the methods **OnTriggerEnter** and **OnTriggerExit**, and we then display the name of the objects that are used to define the trigger area. In both cases, no collision will be detected and the player will be able to walk through the other objects, as these objects will only be acting as triggers.

Note that this script would also work if it was added to the primitive that defines the trigger area.

Detecting Objects With Ray-Casting

As we have seen in the previous sections, you can detect collision with other objects or set triggers. This being said, you may want to be able to detect the presence of objects located far away from the player or the NPC. In this particular case, ray-casting may make more sense than collision or trigger detection.

Ray-casting implies casting a virtual ray in a specific direction and testing whether an object "collides" with the ray. When you design this ray, its origin may differ; sometimes, for example in FPS game, you may want it to originate from the middle of the screen. In other cases, you may prefer the ray to be created just ahead of an NPC so that it can detect objects ahead. So, we will see how each of these can be employed.

Casting a ray from the middle of the screen

This technique is particularly useful when using First-Person Controllers so that the raycast points exactly in the same direction as where the player looks. In this case, we could create a script that is attached to the object **FirstPersonCharacter** (which is a child of the object **FPSController** used for a First-Person Controller). This is very important because the script will be linked to the latter. If you were to add this script to the object **FPSController** instead, an error would occur because this object does not have a camera component, and the script will still need to use this camera.

The following script illustrates how this could be done.

```
void Update ()
{

    RaycastHit hit;

    rayFromPlayer = playersCamera.ScreenPointToRay (new Vector3
(Screen.width/2, Screen.height/2, 0));

    Debug.DrawRay(rayFromPlayer.origin, rayFromPlayer.direction
* 100, Color.red);

    if (Physics.Raycast(rayFromPlayer, out hit, 100))

    {

            print (" The object " + hit.collider.gameObject.name
+" is in front of the player");

    }

}
```

In the previous code, we do the following:

- We initialize our ray defined earlier. This ray will be originating from the camera used for the **First-Person Controller**, from the center of the screen, which is defined by the **x** and **y** coordinates **Screen.width/2** (that is, half of the screen's width) and **Screen.height/2** (that is, half of the screen's height). The **z** coordinate is ignored since we consider the screen as two-dimensional space. So at this stage, we know where the ray will start and, by default, it will point outwards.

- On the next line, we use the static method **DrawRay** and specify three parameters: the origin of the ray, its direction, and its color. By using the syntax **ray.origin** we will start the ray from the middle of the screen. By using the syntax **rayFromPlayer.direction*100**, we specify that the ray's length is 100 meters. This ray can only be seen in the **Scene** view, but not the **Game** view.

- We cast a ray using the keyword **Physics.RayCast**. The method **RayCast** takes three parameters: the ray (**rayFromPlayer**), an object where the information linked to the collision between the ray and another collider is stored (**hit**), and the length of the ray (**100**). The keyword **out** is used so that the information returned about the collision is easily accessible (this is comparable to a type conversion or casting).

- If this ray hits an object (i.e., the collider from an object), we print a message that displays the name of this object. To obtain this name, we access the collider involved in the collision, then the corresponding **GameObject** using the syntax **hit.collider.gameObject**.

The method **Debug.DrawRay** will create a ray that we can see in the scene view and that can be used for debugging purposes to check that a ray effectively points in the right direction. However, **Debug.DrawRay** does not detect collisions with objects. So while it is useful to check the direction of a particular ray in the **Scene** view, this ray needs to be combined to a different method to be able to detect collisions and one of these methods is called **Physics.Raycast**.

Casting a ray from an object

There may be cases when you want to cast a ray from an object. For example, you might want to equip NPCs with the ability to see and detect objects ahead. In this case, you could create a ray that originates just a few centimeters ahead of the NPC and that is cast forward.

The only difference with the previous example would be the creation of the ray; so we would, in this case, replace this line.

```
rayFromPlayer = playersCamera.ScreenPointToRay (new Vector3
(Screen.width/2, Screen.height/2, 0));
```

… with this line …

```
Ray rayFromPlayer = new Ray (transform.position +
transform.forward * 1.5f, transform.forward);
```

In the previous code we create a ray that starts 1.5 meters ahead of the player and that is pointing forward.

WORKING WITH XML FILES

When you are creating scenes procedurally, it may be interesting to save information in an XML file and to access it at run-time. XML files can also be used for data visualization related to weather, financial transactions, scientific measurements, or news information. Many of these XML files are freely available and can be accessed and processed relatively easily. So, for example, you could create a 3D environment that simulates scientific data such as temperatures, or streams in the oceans, and since these files are usually updated on a regular basis, you could provide a 3D application that simulates real life phenomena.

So first, what is an XML file?

XML stands for e**X**tensible **M**arkup **L**anguage. It was originally designed to store data in a way that could be read by both humans and computers. As you will see in the next code examples, these files use the extension **.xml** and have a common structure that makes them easy to read and understand.

Let's look at an XML file that we could create to describe a scene. It could look like the following:

> Please note that, given that you follow simple XML rules, you can create and set a structure of your choice for your XML file, which makes them very versatile.

```xml
<?xml version="1.0" encoding="UTF-8"?>

<game>

     <level number ="1">

          <object name = "wall1" color = "red" location =
"0,0,0" rotation = "0,0,0" scale = "1,2,1">

          </object>

     </level>

     <level number ="2">

     </level>

</game>
```

- So, an XML file includes a succession of nested elements delimited by their tags. For example, in the previous code, the game elements start with **<game>** and ends with **</game>**. Each element also includes attributes. For example, in the previous

[215]

example, we have levels nested within each game elements. For each of these levels, a number is defined. Similarly, for each object within a level, attributes such as **color**, **location** or **scale** are defined also.

- The first line of the XML file is optional, but it is good practice to add it. It basically mentions that the version **1.0** of XML, which is the default encoding for XML, is used and that the encoding used is **UTF8**.

When creating XML documents, there are other rules that must be followed, including:

- Each element is delimited by and includes an opening and a closing tag. As you can see, there is a opening **<game>** tag along with a closing **</game>** tag. The back slash "/" marks a closing tag for an element.

- These tags are case-sensitive which means that using **<game>** followed by **</GAme>** is incorrect; but using **<game>** followed by **</game>** is correct.

- All elements need to be nested properly. For example, the following nesting is correct (e.g., the first tag open is the last tag closed):

```
<game><object></object></game>
```

While the next nesting is not correct:

```
<game><object></game></object>
```

- Elements can have attributes and these must be defined using quotes.

The beauty of this file format is that you can create your own XML files using a structure of your choice to best reflect and serve the requirements of your game or application. You could save information about each scene, about the NPCs (for example, the paths that they can use), or about weapons. This means that you could virtually save any type of information with these files.

Now that the XML format has been explained, let's see how we can read an XML file to create a simple scene.

In the next section, we will:

- Load an XML file.

- Open this document.

- Navigate through each level node or element.

- For each of these nodes, create the corresponding game objects defined for this scene.

First let's look at the XML file that we will be using:

```
<?xml version="1.0" encoding="UTF-8"?>
<game>
    <level number ="1">
        <object name = "wall1" color = "red" location =
"10,0,10" rotation = "0,0,0" scale = "1,2,1">
        </object>
    </level>

    <level number ="2">
<object name = "wall2" color = "red" location = "20,0,10"
rotation = "0,0,0" scale = "1,2,1">
        </object>
    </level>
</game>
```

As you can see in the previous code, the file includes the following:

- A first line with information on the version of XML used along with the encoding type.

- We then define the root node called **game**. This is the node that contains every other node in the XML file.

- For this **game** element (or node), we have two direct children elements called **level**.

- For each **level** element (or node) present in the XML file, we have defined an attribute called **number**. We also added an object to each level with specific attributes called **name**, **color**, **location**, **rotation** and **scale**. The idea here is to define the location and appearance of each object to be included in the scene.

- For each opening tag, we also create a corresponding closing tag (for example **<game>** and **</game>**, **<level>** and **</level>** or **<object>** and **</object>**).

So at this stage, we have defined an XML file that we want to read to be able to create a scene accordingly.

First, we will copy this file from the resource pack to our project:

- If you don't already have a folder called **Resources** within the **Assets** folder in Unity, you can create one using the option **Create | Folder** from the **Project** window.

- You can then copy the file called **scene.xml** from the resource pack to the **Resources** folder in Unity (using drag and drop).

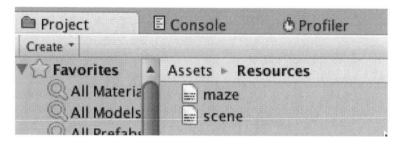

Figure 36: Adding the scene.xml file to the Resources

Next, we will create the code that reads the XML file.

- Please create a new C# script called **GenerateMaze**.

- Open this script in your code editor.

- Add the following code at the beginning of the script **GenerateMaze**:

```
using System.Xml;
```

- This will make it possible to read and process the XML file.

- Add the following lines of code to the **Start** function:

```
TextAsset textAsset = (TextAsset) Resources.Load("scene");
XmlDocument doc = new XmlDocument ();
doc.LoadXml ( textAsset.text );
```

In the previous code:

- We create an object of type **TextAsset**, and it will include the content of the file **scene.xml** that is stored in the **Resources** folder.

- We then create an XML document called **doc**.

- We transfer the text from the file **scene.xml** file to the object called **doc**.

Next, we will read the XML file:

- Please add the following code within the previous conditional statement (just after the previous line):

```
foreach (XmlNode level in doc.SelectNodes("game/level"))
{
    if (level.Attributes.GetNamedItem ("number").Value == "1")
    {
        foreach (XmlNode gameObject in
level.SelectNodes(".//object"))
        {
```

In the previous code:

- We look at each element (or node) of type **level** using the keyword **foreach**. So in other words, within this statement, anytime we read an element of type **level**, it will be referred as **level**.

The keyword foreach can be used to go through each element within a group.

- Then, for this level, we read the values of the attribute called **number**; if it is **1**, then we proceed with the rest of the code. In other words, we only read the content of the first level (or scene). You can, of course, change this code to read the content of **scene2** if you wish, and this is just a way to illustrate how it is possible to focus on the content to be created for a particular level. In our case, this will be the first level.

- For each object node (or element) found in this level, we will then instantiate a corresponding **GameObject**.

- Each of these objects will be referred to as **gameObject** in the rest of the code.

Once we access one of the **GameObjects** defined for level 1, we can then read its attribute and create a corresponding **GameObject** in the scene as follows.

- Please add the following code, just after the previous line.

```
string name, location;

name = gameObject.Attributes.GetNamedItem ("name").Value;

location = gameObject.Attributes.GetNamedItem ("location").Value;

Vector3 v = ConvertStringToVector (location);

GameObject g = (GameObject)Instantiate (wall, v,
Quaternion.identity);

g.name = name;
```

In the previous code, for each relevant node or element:

- We define two string variables called **name** and **location**.

- We then obtain both the **name** and **location** attributes of the objects in the XML file using the method **getNamedItem**.

- We then call a function, that we yet have to define, that will convert the string for the location to a **Vector3** value, so that it can be used to set the location of the new object to be instantiated. At present the location information included in the XML file is a string that includes the **x**, **y** and **z** coordinated, separated by a comma.

- We then instantiate a new object called **wall** at the position defined earlier, and we set its **name** with the name that was defined previously.

To navigate through our XML document, we have used a syntax called **XPath** which includes a set of commands that make it easier to navigate through complex XML documents.

- Please add the following code to your script, so that the conditional statements and the function **Start** are ended and closed properly.

```
            }


        }
    }
```

- So your function **Start** should now look as follows:

```
void Start()
{

    TextAsset textAsset = (TextAsset) Resources.Load("scene");

    XmlDocument doc = new XmlDocument ();

    doc.LoadXml ( textAsset.text );

    foreach (XmlNode level in doc.SelectNodes("game/level"))

    {

        if (level.Attributes.GetNamedItem ("number").Value ==
"1")

        {

            foreach (XmlNode gameObject in
level.SelectNodes(".//object"))

            {

                string name, location;

                name = gameObject.Attributes.GetNamedItem
("name").Value;

                location =
gameObject.Attributes.GetNamedItem ("location").Value;

                Vector3 v = ConvertStringToVector
(location);

                GameObject g = (GameObject)Instantiate
(wall, v, Quaternion.identity);

                g.name = name;

            }

        }

    }
}
```

- Please save your code.

So now, let's look at how we can convert the **location** variable (that is of type **string**) to a vector. To do so, we will use a simple process that involves the following:

- Splitting the string that includes the location (and the three corresponding coordinates), based on the commas that it includes within.

- This should create three different strings, each corresponding respectively to the x, y, and z coordinates.

- We can then convert each of these strings to numbers that can then be used to create a new vector.

I hope this is clear, and the following code should also speak volumes. So please add the following code just before the end of the class:

```
Vector3 ConvertStringToVector(string s)
{
    string [] newString;
    newString = s.Split (new char [] { ',' });
    float x, y, z;
    x = float.Parse (newString[0]);
    y = float.Parse (newString[1]);
    z = float.Parse (newString[2]);
    return new Vector3 (x, y, z);
}
```

In the previous code:

- We declare a method called **ConvertStringToVector**.

- Within this method, we declare a **string** array.

- We then use this array to store the different parts (i.e., coordinates) of the string that we have just split.

- The command **Split** splits the string **s** (that was passed as a parameter). Since **s** consists of a string in the form "**x, y, z**", we specify that the separator used to split this string is a comma. In other words, any part of this string (i.e., the string **s**) that is within (or surrounded by) commas will be used to create a new string variable. In our case, **x** will be used to create a new variable, then **y** will be used to create a new string, and so on.

- So after splitting the string variable **s** we should obtain three **char** variables. These are in turn converted to strings (that is, stored in the variable **newString**), and then to float values (using **float.Parse**).

- A new vector based on these three floats is then created and returned.

You can now save your script.

Before you can play the scene, we just need to do the following:

- Select the object **generateMaze** in the **Hierarchy**.

Once this is done, you can play the scene, and you should see a new **wall** object called **wall1** at the position **(10, 0, 10)** in your scene.

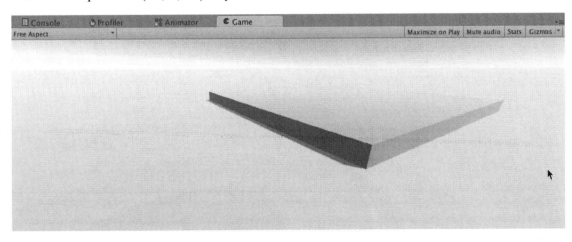

Figure 37: A wall created based on the XML file

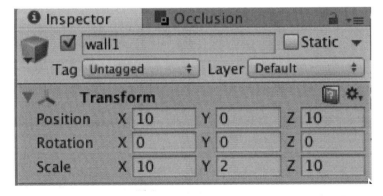

Figure 38: Coordinates of the new wall

ACCESSING RESOURCES FROM YOUR PROJECT (SPRITES)

There are times when you may want to access assets at run time from your script, such as sprites, and in this case, you could do the following:

- Create a folder called **Resources** within the **Assets** folder.

- Within this folder, create a folder with the name of your choice, for example **myFolder**.

- Copy and paste all the sprites that you need in this folder.

- Use a script that includes the following code to use these sprites.

```
Sprite[] allSprites = Resources.LoadAll<Sprite> ("myFolder");
Sprite s1 = allSprites [2];
```

In the previous code:

- We create an array of **Sprites**.

- This array is initialized with the content of the folder **myFolder**. All sprites in this folder are saved in the array called **allSprites**.

- We access the third sprite in the array and save it in the variable called **s1**.

- This sprite can then be used, for example, as an image.

You can, of course, use the method **Resource.Load** to load a specific asset and the same approach applies when accessing files of other types.

SAVING DATA ACROSS SCENES

Quite often, you will need to save data across scenes in your game. However, by default, all objects in the scene are destroyed when loading a new scene. So in this case, you have several choices: (1) to save your game manager and associated scripts and attach them to an object that also includes a script with the method **DontDestroyOnLoad** within (as we have seen previously), (2) use the **Player Preferences**, or (3) use **public static** objects or variables that are shared and accessible throughout your game.

So let's look at the **Player Preferences**. The class **PlayerPrefs** makes it possible to save information that can be accessed throughout the game. This information can consist of variables of type **string**, **int**, or **float**. Any of these values, once set, can be read and modified subsequently. The following script provides an example of how this can be done to save the score across the game regardless of the current scene.

- First, we could set the score from the very first scene as follows.

```
PlayerPrefs.SetInt ("score", 0);
```

In the previous code, we create a variable **score** that will be saved in the **Player Preferences** and initially set to **0**.

- We could then access and update this score from any other scene using this code:

```
int tempScore = PlayerPrefs.GetInt ("score");
tempScore++;
PlayerPrefs.SetInt ("score", tempScore);
```

In the previous code:

- We create a new temporary variable called **tempScore**.

- We then read the value of the **score** variable that is saved in the **Player Preferences** and save it in the variable **tempScore**.

- We increase the variable **tempScore** by one.

- We then update the variable **score** that is saved in the **Player Preferences**.

Note that we could have done the same to save (and read) a string or a float value, using, the methods **PlayerPrefs.GetString/ PlayerPrefs.SetString** or **PlayerPrefs.GetFloat/ PlayerPrefs.SetFloat**, respectively.

USING ATTRIBUTES AND MODIFYING THE INSPECTOR

As you create your games, there will be times when you will want to control some parameters at run-time to perform tests. For example: you may want to be able to modify a variable inside the **Inspector** while the game is running by typing its value or by using a slider to make this easier. In both cases, you will need to modify the **Inspector** and the way data is presented within.

Thankfully, Unity makes it possible for you to perform these changes from your own C# script. The first thing we could do, is to make our variable public, as all public variables are available and modifiable in the **Inspector**.

We could also, in addition, define a range, so that we know that people testing the game within Unity can only modify the values of this variable within a specific range, as illustrated in the following code.

```
[Range(1.0f,10.0f)]
public float myVariable;
```

In the previous code, we use the keyword **Range** followed by values that indicate the range for the variable **myVariable**. The **Inspector** would then look as illustrated in the next figure.

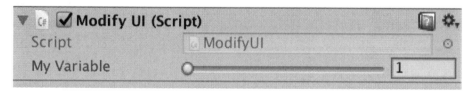

Figure 39: Modifying the Inspector

Next, we could make it possible to display and change the value of private variables. By default, private variables are not displayed in the Inspector, unless they are proceeded by using the attribute **SerializedField** as illustrated in the next code.

```
[SerializeField]
private int myPrivateVariable;
```

This being said, Unity also makes it possible to use attributes to modify the behaviours of variables, classes, or methods, when the scene is not played. For example, the following attributes can be used at run-time:

- **HideInInspector**: can be used to hide some variables in the Inspector; for example, a variable might be public but you may not want to make it possible to readjust its value in the **Inspector**.

```
public class TestSerialized : MonoBehaviour
{

    [HideInInspector]

    public int myPrivateVariable;//this variable will be hidden

    public Vector3 test;
```

- **Serializable**: this attribute gives the opportunity to serialize a class, so that member variables content can be displayed in the **Inspector**.

```
[System.Serializable]

public class TestSerialized : MonoBehaviour
{
// All public member variables will be visible in the Inspector

    public int myPrivateVariable;

    public Vector3 test;
```

- **ExecuteInEditMode**: this attribute makes it possible to execute a script even in edit mode. Please use this attribute carefully as any of the changes made will be permanent in this case. When things are changed at run-time, your scene will be back to normal when your stop playing it; however, when you perform actions from your code that is executed in edit mode (i.e., with the attribute **ExecuteInEditMode**) you may need to be careful as the changes made from your script will be permanent.

ENUMS

Enums can be employed when you need a label for some variables or when some variables can only include a small and finite numbers of values. It usually also makes it possible to avoid errors related to parameters passed to methods. First let's look at how enums are declared.

An enum consists of a list of labels, each of them will correspond to an integer value. The first parameter will correspond to 0, the second parameter to 1, as illustrated in the next code snippet.

```
public enum NPC_TYPE {GUARD, CHASER, IDLE};
void Start ()
{
    print ( NPC_TYPE.GUARD);// This will print NPC_TYPE.GUARD
    print ( (int) NPC_TYPE.GUARD);// This will print 0
}
```

In the previous code:

- We declare an **enum** type called **NPC_TYPE**. It includes three different identifiers (or labels) called **GUARD**, **CHASER**, and **IDLE**.

- We then print one of the identifiers in the method **Start**.

- We also print the value (as an integer) of this identifier.

So why would you use enums?

This is a good question because a similar feature could be achieved by just creating final variables. Well, it may be the case that you would like to limit the range of the variables employed for a particular function. For example, you may create a function for which you would like the parameters to be part of a small number of values and be able to check before compiling that the parameters passed to this function match this range. So let's look at the following code to see how this could be implemented.

```
public enum NPC_TYPE {GUARD, CHASER, IDLE};

void Start ()

{

    myFunction (NPC_TYPE.GUARD);

    //myFunction (99); won't work

}

void myFunction (NPC_TYPE type)

{

    print ("Type" + type);

}
```

In the previous code:

- We are declaring the same **enum** type as before.

- We also create a function called **myFunction** that takes a parameter of type **NPC_Type**; in other words, the parameter should be one of the identifiers from the enum type **NPC_TYPE**.

- Now we call the function **myFunction** and pass the parameter **NPC_TYPE.GUARD**, and this will work (i.e., no errors in the **Console** window); this is because the type of the argument passed to the function is **NPC_TYPE.GUARD**, which matches the type required by the function.

- However, you can see that if we had, instead, called the function using this code...

```
myFunction (99)
```

...it would not have worked and an error would have been generated. This is because, in this case, we would have passed a parameter of type **integer**, instead of **NPC_TYPE**.

So by using **Enums**, we have limited the type and range of the arguments passed to the method, and as a result, the method is safer to use because we know exactly what numbers will be passed to this function. Of course, this can only be applied when dealing with a small number of possible values, but it is very effective in that it makes your code less prone to errors.

SCRIPTABLE OBJECTS

Scriptable objects are extremely well suited for saving and accessing complex data, as for XML file.

Scriptable objects are essentially data containers deriving from the Unity class **Object**. They can't be attached to a game object (because they don't derive from the class **MonoBehaviour**). However, they can be created at run time and instances of these objects can be saved as assets.

So a scriptable object can provide a template for the data that you would like to save in your game. In the next section, we will see how it is possible to create such classes and to also instantiate these in order to have and access formatted data that can be employed in your game. So let's go ahead!

Let's say that you would like to save information about a specific type of NPC. In this case, we could create the following script that will be a template for the data to be saved.

```csharp
using System.Collections;

using System.Collections.Generic;

using UnityEngine;


[CreateAssetMenu()]//this is so that this option/asset appears in
the Inspector
public class ScriptableObjectExample : ScriptableObject {


    public string npcName ="NPC1";

    public int xpLevel = 12;

    public int nbWeapons = 3;

}
```

In the previous code:

- We add the attribute **[CreateAssetMenu]**. This attribute will, once our class has been compiled, make it possible to create assets (instances of this class) from the **Asset** menu in Unity.

- We then declare our class and specify that it is **Scriptable**.

- Once this is done, we declare several member variables such as the name of the NPC, its XP level, as well as the number of weapons it has. You could, of course, use any other variables of your choice.

- Note that the variables are public so that they can be modified later on in the **Inspector**.

Next, we could create another script, attached to an empty object, that will be employed to instantiate our Scriptable object as follows.

```
using System.Collections;

using System.Collections.Generic;

using UnityEngine;


public class UseScriptableObject : MonoBehaviour {

    public ScriptableObjectExample soe;

    void Start () {}

    void Update () {        }

}
```

In the previous script, we just declare an instance of the class **ScriptaleObjectExample** created earlier.

If you save both scripts, you should see the that the following menu is now available in Unity by selecting: **Assets | Create | Scriptable Object Example**. This is thanks to the attribute **[CreateAssetMenu]** created in the previous class.

Now that we can see that a new menu is available, there are a few things that we can customize for this menu, and this can be done by modifying the class **ScriptableObjectExample** as follows.

```
[CreateAssetMenu(fileName="NPCInfo", menuName="NPC/details", order=1)]

public class ScriptableObjectExample : ScriptableObject {
```

In the previous code:

- We specify a name for the corresponding menu.

- We also specify an order in this menu.

- As a result, after saving your script, if you look at Unity's **Assets** menu, you should see a menu called **Assets | Create | NPC | details**.

- If you select the menu **Assets | Create | NPC | details**, you should be able to create a data file based on this scriptable class called **NPCInfo** (as defined in the previous script).

Figure 40: Instantiating a new Scriptable object

By clicking on this new asset called **NPCInfo** and after looking at the **Inspector** window, you should be able to see all the public variables that we have previously defined for the Scriptable object, as illustrated in the next figure.

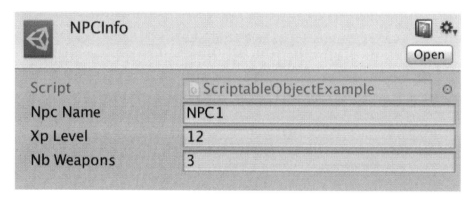

Figure 41: Looking at the properties of the new asset

To be able to use this new asset, we just need to do the following:

- Modify the script **UseScriptableObject** as follows.

```
void Start () {

    if (soe.xpLevel == 12) print ("Powerful NPC");

}
```

- Select the empty object linked to the script **UseScriptableObject** in the **Project** view, and drag and drop the asset **NPCInfo** to the empty field called **soe** available from the script **UserScriptableObject**, as illustrated in the next figure.

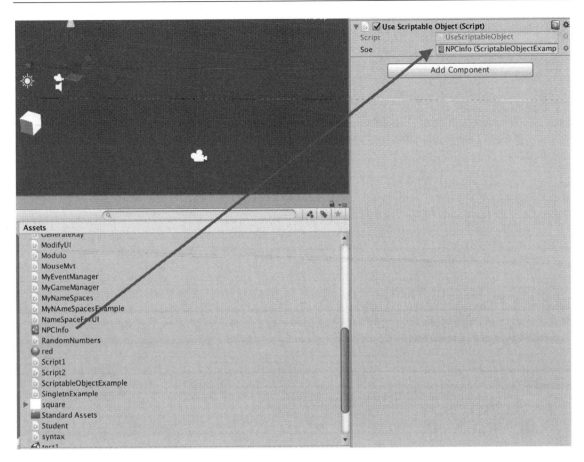

Figure 42: Assigning the data object

To make this more interesting, we could just specify a series of positions in our data file that need to be employed to instantiate objects, and we could proceed as follows.

- Please modify the script called **ScriptableObjectExample** as follows (new code in bold):

```
public int nbWeapons = 3;
public Vector3 [] wayPoints;
public bool canPatrol = true;
```

- Modify the script **UseScriptableObject** as follows (new code is in bold).

```
if (soe.canPatrol)
{
    foreach (Vector3 wayPoint in soe.wayPoints)
    {
        GameObject g = new GameObject ();
        g.transform.SetPositionAndRotation (wayPoint,
Quaternion.identity);
        g.name = "wayPoint";
    }
}
```

In the previous code:

- We check whether the variable **soe.canPatrol** is true.

- We then loop through the array of waypoints.

- For each waypoint found, we instantiate an empty object.

Once this is done, we just need to create a new asset based on the amended **Scriptable** object as follows.

- Select **Assets | Create | NPC | Details** from the top menu in Unity.

- Rename the new asset created as **NPCInfo2**.

- Select the asset **NPCInfo2** in the **Hierarchy** window, and, using the **Inspector**, modify the size of the array to **4**, as illustrated in the next figure.

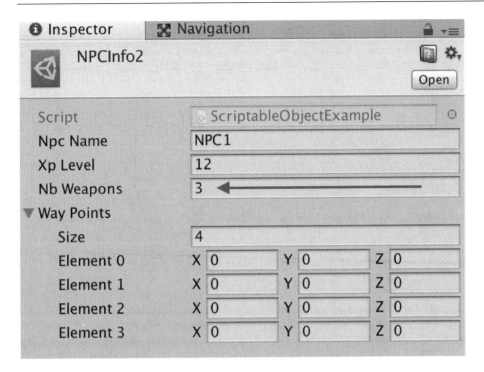

Figure 43: Modifying the new asset (part 1)

- Modify each element of the array as illustrated in the next figure (that is, **Element 0**, **Element 1**, **Element 2**, etc.).

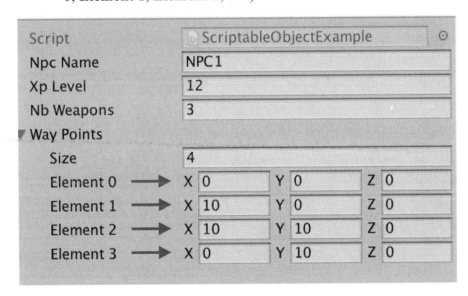

Figure 44: Modifying the new asset (part 2)

- Drag and drop this new data file to the field **soe**.

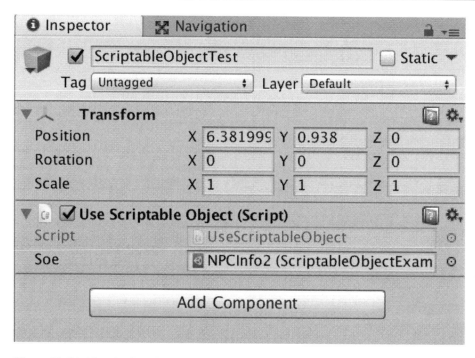

Figure 45: Linking the data file to the empty object

As you play the scene, you should see that **4** different empty objects have been created.

So **Scriptable** objects are very useful, as they can, as for XML files, store information that can be used in Unity. One of the key advantages, compared to XML files, is that they don't need to be parsed, so **Scriptable** objects are easier to access and to manipulate in Unity.

LEVEL ROUNDUP

In this chapter, we have learned more about using C# in Unity. Along the way we also looked at key methods that are commonly employed in games for collision detection, reading files, or detecting the players' inputs. We also looked at more intermediate concepts such as scriptable objects. So, we have, again, covered some significant ground compared to the last chapter.

Checklist

You can consider moving to the next chapter if you can do the following:

- Know how to detect objects based on collision or raycast.

- Know how to play audio files.

- Understand the advantage of using Scriptable objects compared to XML files.

Quiz

Now, let's check your knowledge! Please answer the following questions or specify if these statements are either correct or incorrect. The solutions are on the next page.

1. It is possible to detect collision with an object using the method **OnCollisionEnter**.

2. The method **GetComponent** can be used to access a component from a **GameObject**.

3. Casting helps to convert a variable (or to ensure that it belongs) to a certain type or class.

4. The methods **Start** and **Update** are usually added by default to new scripts in Unity.

5. It is possible to look for particular objects in the scene, from a script, based on their name or tag.

6. Only scripts attached to the same object can communicate and exchange data.

7. Any object included in the scene can be activated or deactivated from a script.

8. The class **Input** makes it possible to detect keystrokes.

9. Scriptable objects can be used to store data.

10. Enums make it possible to avoid bugs before run-time.

Quiz Solutions

Now, let's check if you have answered the questions correctly.

1. True.

2. True.

3. True.

4. True.

5. True.

6. False.

7. True.

8. True.

9. True.

10. True.

Challenge 1

Now that you have managed to complete this chapter and that you know how to use several C# methods in Unity, you could try the following:

- Create a Scriptable object and use it to implement a simple inventory system for an NPC.

- Use attributes for some of your variables so that testers can modify these with a slider.

5

OPTIMIZING THE STRUCTURE AND EFFICIENCY OF YOUR CODE

In this section, we will start to look at several ways to optimize your code so that it can be both efficient and easily maintained over time.

After completing this chapter, you will be able to:

- Code defensively to make your game faster and your code more efficient.

- Use common structures based on well-known design patterns.

- Know and use best programming practices to make your code easily maintainable over time.

- Organize your script so that it becomes easy for you to expand your projects without headaches.

The code solutions for this chapter are in the **resource pack** that you can download by following the instructions included in the section entitled "Support and Resources for this Book".

CODING TIPS TO PROGRAM DEFENSIVELY

In this section, we will now try to see how you can use very simple tips so that your code makes for a faster game and a more efficient game logic.

When it comes to scripting, even at an intermediate level, there are a few things that you can do to make sure that your code is lean and efficient, including:

- Using the methods **Update** and **FixedUpdate** wisely.

- Deactivating unnecessary scripts temporarily.

- Removing overridable methods.

- Using search functions wisely.

- Spawning objects and using prefabs.

- Using public variables wisely.

- Using strings sparingly.

The next sections will explore each of these principles in detail.

USING UPDATE AND FIXEDUPDATE

Sone functions such as **FixedUpdate** or **Update** can be called several times per seconds from Unity. So it is good practice not to process too much code in these methods, unless necessary, as it would slow down your game otherwise. The former (**FixedUpdate**) can be called 10 times per second, while the latter (**Update**) is called every time your screen is refreshed. So, it is better not to add code in these methods, unless necessary. If you really have to use one of these methods, then the **Update** method may be best.

So the following code...

```
public void Update()
{
    print("Starting the game");
}
```

... could be replaced by this code.

```
public void Start()
{
    print("Starting the game");
}
```

This is because the **Start** method will only be called once (at the start of the scene) and because the print statement does not need to be used every frame.

DEACTIVATING SCRIPTS THAT ARE NOT USED

In addition to choosing in which method to execute your code, it is also good to temporarily deactivate the scripts that may not be used in your game. For example, some objects linked to NPCs may not be used until the player is close to these NPCs. In this case, you can deactivate the script after creating a reference to it. For example, let's imagine that the following code is part of a script called **NPC.cs** that is linked to an NPC.

```
void Start()
{
    GameObject player = GameObject.find("player");
}
void Update()
{
    if (Vector3.Distance(gameObect.transform, player.transform)
< 1.0f) Fire();
}
public void Fire()
{
...

}
```

You could activate or deactivate the previous script as follows:

```
void Start()
{
     GameObject NPC = GameObject.Find("npc");
     NPC.GetComponent<NPC>().active = false;
}
void Update()
{
     if (Vector3.Distance(gameObect.transform, NPC.transform) <
1.0f) ActivateNPC();
}
public void ActivateNPC()
{
     NPC.GetComponent<NPC>().active = false;
}
```

In the previous code:

- We create a reference to the object npc, and then a reference to its component called **NPC** (which is a script).

- We then temporarily deactivate the script called **NPC**.

- In the **Update** function, we check the distance between the NPC and the player.

- If the distance is less than 1 meter, we then activate the script called **NPC** from the NPC.

REMOVING OVERRIDABLE METHODS

As you may have already noticed, new C# files in Unity usually extend the **MonoBehaviour** class, which means that a new class will inherit some properties from the base class (that is, the class **MonoBehaviour**), and include methods that can be overridden.

This is the case, for example, for the methods **Start** and **Update**. Now, when you create a new C# script, it usually includes an empty **Update** method by default, as described in the next code snippet;

```
Update ()
{

}
```

It is instinctive (and understandable) to think that, because it is empty, it does not do anything. However, the issue is that, whenever your script includes an **Update** method, it is added to a list of scripts to be called every frame by Unity, even if the **Update** method does not include any code. So it is good to remove any empty "magic" method from your code (such as **Start** or **Update**, etc.) when they are not used.

USING SEARCH FUNCTIONS WISELY

At this stage of your journey through Unity, you may already have used built-in methods such as **GameObject.Find** to locate and refer to specific objects in your scene. This is a function that searches for a particular object in the scene. These search functions are usually costly in terms of time and performance because every time you search for an object, Unity looks through all the objects in the scene to find a particular object, and for this reason, it is good to use these functions as little as possible, or at least in methods that are not called often (that is, especially <u>not</u> in the **Update** or **FixedUpdate** methods). This being said, a better way to do use search functions is to look for and "cache" an object once (in the **Start** method, for example) and then make a reference to the object found, that can then be used later without the need to search for the object again. This is illustrated in the next code snippet.

```
void Start()
{
    GameObject NPC = GameObject.Find("npc");
}
void Update()
{
    if (...) NPC.transform.position ...
}
```

In the previous code:

- We look for the object called **npc** and store it in a variable. The function **Update** then uses the variable created (that is, a reference to the object **npc**).

[245]

If you really need to look for an object every frame, you may use the method **GameObject.FindWithTag** instead, which is less computer intensive.

SPAWNING OBJECTS AND USING PREFABS:

As you already know, prefabs are comparable to reusable templates that you can use to create similar objects from your scripts, hence making it faster to add and update similar objects in your scene. Changes applied to a prefab are applied to all objects (or instances) based on this prefab, so it is often good to use prefabs for all objects employed in your scene. By using prefabs, modifying objects is made easier as only one prefab needs to be modified for all related instances/objects to be modified at the same time.

So, it makes sense to convert your objects to prefabs as much as possible, to save you some time.

Another aspect of prefabs is that, as you spawn prefabs, it may be difficult to see them in the **Hierarchy** window. So a good practice is to add them to a parent object. For example, you could create an empty object called **NPC**, and then when the NPC has been spawned, set its parent as the object **NPC** using the method **transform.SetParent**, as described in the next code snippet.

```
using UnityEngine;
using System.Collections;

public class CreatePrefabs : MonoBehaviour {

    public GameObject parent, myPrefab;
    void Start()
    {
        parent = GameObject.Find("NPC");
        GameObject t = (GameObject) Instantiate (myPrefab, new
Vector3(0,0,0), Quaternion.identity);
        t.transform.SetParent (parent.transform);
    }
    void Update()
    {
    }
}
```

Finally, you may decide to design a game where objects are loaded from the previous scene such as the GUI, the players, or the NPCs (that is, using the method **DontDestroyOnLoad**).; however, when you test your game, this will probably be done per scene. In other words, your game could be designed to load **scene1**, and then **scene2** (with objects from the previous scene), and so on. However, you may want to only load **scene2** for testing purposes, with no previous scenes pre-loaded (for example **scene1**). If this is the case, you may run into a problem whereby **scene2** is trying to use objects that have not yet been instantiated, because **scene1** has not been loaded just before **scene2**. So in this case, it could be useful to do the following:

- Check if a particular object is present in the scene (or not null).

- If this is the case, then perform an action.

```
myObject = GameObject.Find ("test");


if (myObjet != null)
{

    ...

}
```

USING PUBLIC VARIABLES

You will probably use public variables in your scripts, possibly so that they can be modified using the **Inspector**. However, if a variable is not meant to be used and modified in the **Inspector**, it is better not to declare it as public. If you really need to use a public variable, but not available of it in the **Inspector**, then you can also use the keyword **HideInInspector**, as described in the next code snippet.

```
[HideInInspector]
public string myVariable = "My Var";
```

USING TEXT SPARINGLY

If you are using a considerable amount of text in your game (e.g., for dialogues or to describe objects), it is good to store this text in a file (e.g., separate file) so that it can be loaded and read externally, rather than entering the text in the **Inspector** manually. This is also valid for games that need to be localized (that is, translated in different languages). In this case, you could have different files for each language considered. This can be achieved through an XML file, for example.

MONITORING AND IMPROVING PERFORMANCES (PROFILING)

When your game has been developed, and before trying to optimize the code, it is always good to profile your game, that is, to identify areas that may need optimization. The process often involves profiling, modifying the code, and profiling again to ensure that the changes made were successful.

Discovering the Profiler

The **Profiler** is a tool provided by Unity so that you can see and (correct) part of the game that may be too computer-intensive, and that may slow-down the gameplay significantly. The **Profiler** window can be opened in Unity using the shortcut **CTRL + 7** or by selecting the menu **Window | Profile**.

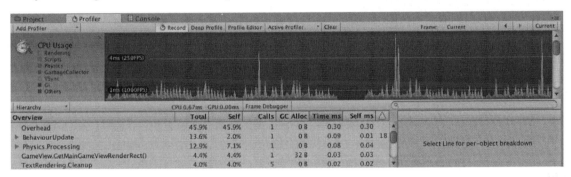

Figure 46: The Profiler window

The **Profiler** usually includes three difference areas:

- A top area with graphics.

- An area located in the bottom-left part of the **Profiler** (**Overview**).

- An area in the bottom-right part of the **Profiler** where information can be displayed for specific objects.

By default, the **Profiler** measures several aspects of a game, including: CPU, GPU, Rendering, Memory, Audio, Physics, Physics2D, Network Messages, and Network Operations. You can see these by scrolling up and down within the **Overview** window.

The images to the left of the **Overview** area provide information on specific aspects of the game, and each of these are color-coded. For example, and as illustrated in the next figure, for the section **CPU Usage**: green is used for **Rendering** and blue is used for **Scripts**.

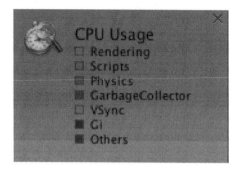

Figure 47: Filtering the information displayed (part 1)

You can also switch any of these sections or aspects **ON** or **OFF** by clicking on the corresponding box to the left of its corresponding label. For example, in the next figure, information on **Rendering** and **Scripts** has been switched off as a black square is displayed to the left of each of these labels.

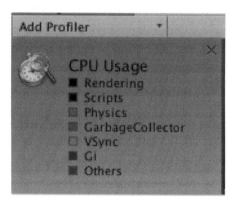

Figure 48: Filtering the information displayed (part 2)

The data provided in the bottom-left corner of the **Profiler** window varies overtime. However, it is possible to display information for a specific frame (that is, a particular point in time) by clicking in the graphics section. Clicking on the graphics will pause the game, and you will be able to access information at a specific frame. The frame number is also displayed in the top right corner of the **Profiler** in this case.

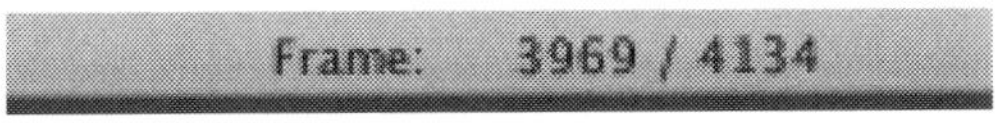
Frame: 3969 / 4134

Figure 49: Displaying the frame number

You can expand any of the items present in the **Profiler**'s hierarchy, and you can also look for a particular item using the search field included in the **Overview** window. However, this will work only when the game is stopped (that is, when profiling and performance recording are stopped). In the next figures, we can see that, by searching for the word **planet**, the results provide us with the methods included in the class **Planet**.

planet

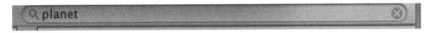

Figure 50: Specifying a word to search for

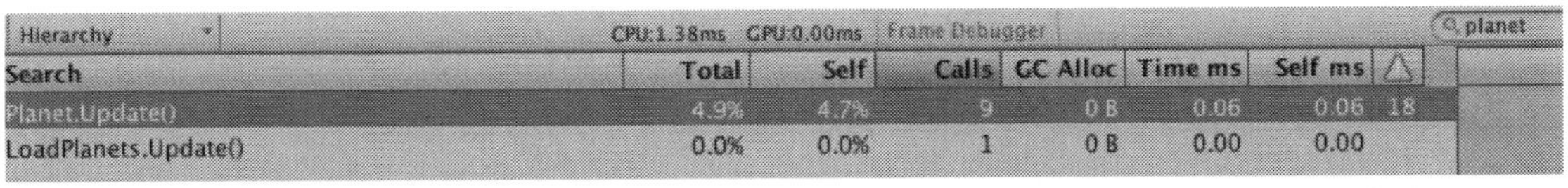
Hierarchy
CPU:1.38ms GPU:0.00ms
Frame Debugger
planet
Search
Total
Self
Calls
GC Alloc
Time ms
Self ms
Planet.Update() 4.9% 4.7% 9 0 B 0.06 0.06 18
LoadPlanets.Update() 0.0% 0.0% 1 0 B 0.00 0.00

Figure 51: Results from the search

> The warning column (that is, the last column to the right) and symbolized by a warning sign, is used in the **Profiler** to specify whether part of the code is likely to cause issues in terms of performance (for example, memory allocation).

Note that you can also use the **Deep Profiler** to display more information, by clicking on the icon called **Deep Profile**, as described on the next figure.

Profiler
Record
Deep Profile
(120FPS)

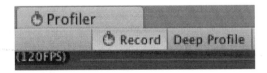

Figure 52: Selecting the Deep Profile option

When you click on this option, a warning window usually appears, and you can select to **Reload**.

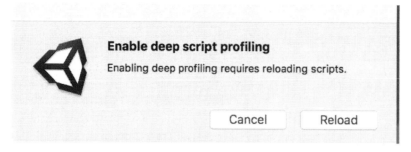

Figure 53: Enabling deep script profiling

Now, in the **Overview** window that is within the **Profiler**, the following columns are available:

- **Total**: the total time it takes to call a block of instruction (including the time required to call other instructions from this block of instruction). For example, it may take a few milliseconds to call the method **Update**. However, this method might, in turn, call other functions.

- **Self**: The time it takes to call a block of instructions.

- **Calls**: Number of calls. For example, a block of instruction may be called once or twice per frame.

- **Time (ms)**: The time it took to execute a particular method or piece of code.

- **GC** (garbage collection): this indicates if the garbage collector has been called. As we will see later, the garbage collector is there to manage our memory (for variables stored in the heap) efficiently. While it does a good job at managing the memory, calling the GC does use some CPU. So we would typically code in a way that would result in a low number of calls to the GC, as much as possible.

> One of the interesting things with the **Profiler** window, is that you can display this information in ascending or descending order for each column (e.g., calls, gc, time, etc.) by clicking on the corresponding label at the top of the column. This could help you to identify key issues related to garbage collection or time.

One of the most important parameters for now will be **Time**, as it indicates how much time will be required to execute parts of our code. In the next example, we will see how some simple coding tweaks can affect the time it takes to complete a function.

Let's create a new script called **TestProfiler.**

- Please create a new scene.

- Create a new C# script.

- Rename it **TestProfiler**.

- Add the following line at the start of the class (new code in bold).

```
public class TestProfiler : MonoBehaviour
{
    int temp = 0;
```

- Please add the following code to the **Update** function:

```
void Update ()
{
    if (temp++ == 5)
    {
        print ("hello World");
        temp = 0;
    }
}
```

- Please create an empty object, rename it (for example **performance**), and attach the script **TestProfiler** to it.

- If we play the scene and run the **Profiler**, we can now see spikes.

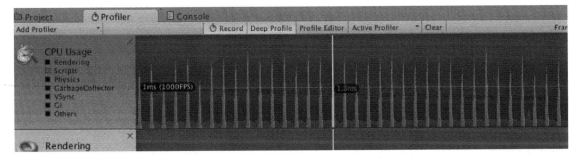

Figure 54: Spikes for CPU usage

Note that you can, as demonstrated in the previous figure, just display information linked to **Scripts** by only selecting the option labelled **Scripts** on the left hand-side of the window, for clarity.

- Some of these spikes correspond to the call to the function **Update**.

- If we click on one of these spikes, and look at the **Overview** window, we can see one of the functions responsible for the spikes.

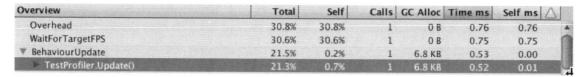

Overview	Total	Self	Calls	GC Alloc	Time ms	Self ms
Overhead	30.8%	30.8%	1	0 B	0.76	0.76
WaitForTargetFPS	30.6%	30.6%	1	0 B	0.75	0.75
▼ BehaviourUpdate	21.5%	0.2%	1	6.8 KB	0.53	0.00
▶ TestProfiler.Update()	21.3%	0.7%	1	6.8 KB	0.52	0.01

Figure 55: Identifying "costly" functions

Note that while the game is paused (or when you have clicked on the graphics part of the Profiler), you can move the cursor to the left or to the right by using the arrow keys on your keyboard. This makes it possible to browse through the profiling information recorded overtime.

- In this case, it took 0.52 milliseconds to execute the code. Note that this time may vary for each spike, as the CPU may be faster or slower at executing this code as it may also be busy performing other tasks at the same time.

- You may also notice the Garbage Collection allocation (GB) of 6.8kb. As you can see, garbage collection needs to be kept to a minimum as it takes resources from the CPU, and we will learn more about garbage collection in the next sections.

- The number of calls is also an important factor, as more calls usually involve more resources. The more often the code is called, and the more resources will be required. Calls usually correspond to the number of time a piece of code is called during a frame. So for example, if we attach the previous script twice to an empty object called **performance**, the number of calls will be doubled, as illustrated on the next figure. So, it is a good idea to ensure that a script is not attached twice to the same object.

Hierarchy	▾		CPU:5.20ms GPU:0.00ms	Frame Debugger		
Overview	Total	Self	Calls	GC Alloc	Time ms	Self ms
▼ BehaviourUpdate	61.9%	0.1%	1	13.4 KB	3.22	0.01
▼ Profiler.Update()	61.8%	0.0%	2	13.4 KB	3.21	0.00
▼ MonoBehaviour.print()	61.7%	0.0%	2	13.4 KB	3.21	0.00
▶ Debug.Log()	61.7%	0.0%	2	13.4 KB	3.21	0.00

Figure 56: Increased number of calls

The same would happen if we included four **print** statements in our code. For example, if we modify the **Update** function as described in the next code snippet, and run the scene again…

```
void Update ()
{
    if (temp++ == 5)

    {
        print ("hello World");

        print ("hello World");

        print ("hello World");

        print ("hello World");

        temp = 0;

    }

}
```

... the **Profiler** window should display that for a single frame, the **Update** function has been accessed twice (that is, because the script is added twice to the object), and that the **print** function was called four times.

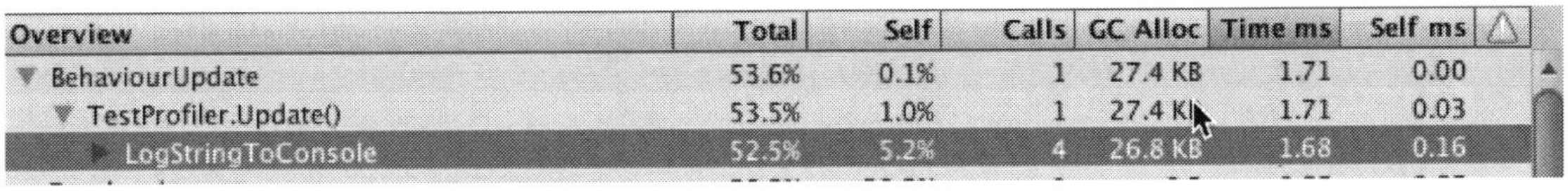

Overview	Total	Self	Calls	GC Alloc	Time ms	Self ms	△
▼ BehaviourUpdate	53.6%	0.1%	1	27.4 KB	1.71	0.00	▲
▼ TestProfiler.Update()	53.5%	1.0%	1	27.4 K	1.71	0.03	
▶ LogStringToConsole	52.5%	5.2%	4	26.8 KB	1.68	0.16	

Figure 57: printing to the Console window

Garbage collection is important as it manages your memory. So the purpose of optimizing your performance is that the Garbage Collector is called as least as possible, hence freeing-up some CPU for other processes. The call to garbage collection can be triggered by specific code. In other words, depending on how the code is written, we can, in some cases, limit or decrease the number of times the garbage collector is called. The ability to decrease the call to the Garbage Collector (GC) is usually linked to good programming practices. So, in the next section we will see how some key coding practices can be used to avoid (excessive) garbage collection.

To make it easier to look for a particular function or method, you can search the **Profiler** window; however, the recording mode has to be stopped before searches can be performed. For example, we could do the following:

- Run the scene with the code we have used previously.

- Stop the scene (at this stage the recording for the profiler has stopped).

- Click on the **Profiler** window.

- The window may look as follows:

Overview	Total	Self	Calls	GC Alloc	Time ms	Self ms
▶ BehaviourUpdate	53.6%	0.1%	1	27.4 KB	1.71	0.00
Overhead	20.3%	20.3%	1	0 B	0.65	0.65
WaitForTargetFPS	15.4%	15.4%	1	0 B	0.49	0.49
▶ Camera.Render	3.0%	0.5%	1	0 B	0.09	0.01
▶ Physics.Processing	2.2%	1.2%	1	0 B	0.07	0.03
Profiler.FinalizeAndSendFrame	1.4%	1.4%	1	0 B	0.04	0.04
GameView.GetMainGameViewRenderRect()	0.8%	0.8%	1	32 B	0.02	0.02
ProcessRemoteInput	0.5%	0.5%	1	0 B	0.01	0.01
AudioManager.Update	0.3%	0.3%	1	0 B	0.01	0.01

Figure 58: Displaying information without filtering

Then enter part of the name of our class in the **Profiler**'s search field

Figure 59: Using the Profiler's search field

The **Profiler** window should now have filtered the entries to display this content instead.

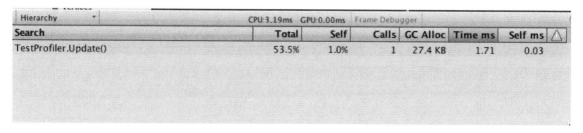

Hierarchy			CPU:3.19ms GPU:0.00ms	Frame Debugger		
Search	**Total**	**Self**	**Calls**	**GC Alloc**	**Time ms**	**Self ms**
TestProfiler.Update()	53.5%	1.0%	1	27.4 KB	1.71	0.03

Figure 60: Filtering the output from the profiler window

As you can see, only access to methods within our class **TestProfiler** are displayed.

> Note that we can also obtain data from and write information about the **Profiler**, using the class **Profiler**.

For example, the method **Profiler.usedHeapSize** can be used to display the heap size used by the game. We will explain the concept of the heap later on, but for now, let's just say that it is some memory allocated to our game where some classes or objects are stored. We could use the method **Profiler.usedHeapSize** to display it before and after a specific code, and to see how costly it is in terms of performance.

For example, we could write the following code in the class **TestProfiler**:

```
print ("Before:"+ Profiler.usedHeapSize);
if (temp++ == 5)
{
    print ("hello World");
    print ("hello World");
    print ("hello World");
    print ("hello World");
    temp = 0;
}
print ("After:"+ Profiler.usedHeapSize);
```

In the previous example, we print the value of the heap size before and after we print the message "**hello World**" four times.

OPTIMIZING GARBAGE COLLECTION AND MEMORY USE

So how can you write code that needs less garbage collection?

In the next sections we will see how it is possible to optimize our code so that data is stored and accessed faster, and also so that garbage collection is either used to a minimum (hence freeing up some CPU) or used more efficiently. The bulk of our work, if we want to optimize our code, will be to avoid garbage collection, as it uses a significant amount of resources. Before considering this code, we will first get to understand a bit better how memory is managed and how data is stored in your game.

MANAGING MEMORY WITH HEAP AND STACK

When a variable is created, its name, type, and values are usually stored in the RAM (Random Memory Access) of your computer (that is, it can also be saved in the CPU cache). However, the location where these will be stored will depend on the variable type. Depending on its type, a variable will be saved in what is called the **heap** or the **stack**. So what are these?

The stack is a type of memory that is used when a function or block of instructions is employed. In this case, for example, temporary variables are stored, until the function (or block of code) is exited. Let's look at the next piece of code:

```
public void testMemory
{
    int i = 0;
    int j = 2;
}
```

In the previous code, the variable **i** is declared inside the method **testMemory**; it is a local (hence temporary) variable that will be stored in the stack when the function is accessed. Once we exit the function, this variable will be deleted (or discarded) from the stack, so that the stack can be used for other methods and corresponding temporary variables. The stack usually has a fixed size (this is often referred as **static memory allocation**), and its name is related to the fact that items are stored in it in a way that can be compared to a stack.

Let's imagine that you have several books that you want to stack together. As you add books to the stack, the very first book that you added to the stack is at the bottom of the pile (or stack), and the very last object added to the pile will be at the top of the stack. As you want to remove objects from the pile, the last object added to the pile (or stack) will be the first object to be removed. In computer terms it is called LIFO (Last-In-First-Out). So in our case, as the function **testMemory** is called, the variable **i** is created and stored in the stack, and so is the variable **j**. As we exit the method **testMemory**, the last variable created (**j**) is destroyed (that is, removed from the stack) and then the variable **i** is also destroyed (or removed from the stack).

So, as you can see, using this principle, it is very easy to keep track of the items added to the stack and to remove them as they are no longer needed. Using a stack for variables is very efficient in terms of memory allocation, especially when no garbage collection is required as the memory allocation is managed automatically and simply for the stack. So, using the stack makes a lot of sense.

Now, there are variables that will, by default, be added to the stack, these are value types variables and include most primitive and basic data types such as **int**, **structs**, **double**, **float**, **char**, **bool**, **Color**, or **Vector3**. Arrays are an exception in that they are not saved in the stack. Primitive data types are very basic in the sense that they contain information related to only themselves, and they usually occupy a small amount of memory (such as a few bytes).

The stack has a static size, and this is the reason why, when we create a variable of a primitive type, it is referred as **static memory allocation**. Now, because these items are relatively small, it has a small cost to copy them on the fly to the stack. However, this may not be the case if we were to deal with bigger data. You could compare it to leaving your apartment every day, versus moving-out every day. While the former could be done very frequently and quickly, because it does not demand much resources, the latter would become quite exhausting if it were to be done every day (because of the number of items to be moved in this case). So we need to find a solution for this: and the solution, in terms of memory management, is called the **heap**.

USING THE HEAP

The heap is used for what is called **dynamic memory allocation**, for example, when you instantiate classes (for example, by using the keyword **new**). The heap has the ability to expand and change its size to accommodate the data stored within. Classes and objects, by definition, are more complex than primitive types because they refer to other variables. For example, we could have a class called **Car** that includes information about a car: its color, its size, or its name. In this particular case, instantiating a car object will also mean keeping track of the variables within the class (i.e., member variables or methods), and not just one variable (as we would for primitive data types). So because of the complexity and the size associated, we would save this data in the heap. Now, the only issue with the heap is that memory is not managed as easily as for the stack (i.e., LIFO); in this case (i.e., for the heap), the garbage collection is needed to tidy-up and to make sure that memory slots are freed-up when they are not used anymore; and in this case, using the garbage collector has a cost in terms of performances. Variables saved in the heap are usually referred as **reference types**; this is because, when these variables are created, a reference (a pointer) is created in the stack, and then the data related to the variable is stored in the heap. The references are managed in the exact same way as value types variable. This is illustrated in the next example:

```
Class Testperf
{

    public void test()
    {

        MyClass mc1 = new MyClass();

        MyClass mc2 = mc // a reference

    }

}
```

- In the previous code, a new object **mc1** is declared and created. Because it is an instance of a class, it is stored in the heap (let's called it **obj1**).

- A new object **mc2** is declared; however, because we don't use the keyword **new**, a reference is created in the stack to the object **obj1** previously created in the heap. In this case, we save some memory allocation (and garbage collection) because the second object is not created in the heap, but instead a reference is created to the corresponding object.

> While value type variables are not usually garbage-collected; if they are member variables, then they will be collected (as they belong to the class).

Let's consider the following examples:

```
Class TestPerf
{

    public int test;

}
```

In the previous code, **test** is a member variable of type **int**, which is a basic type; although this is a basic type, it will be garbage-collected because it is a member variable.

```
Class TestPerf
{
    public void MyMethod()
    {
        int test;
    }
}
```

In the previous code, **test** is a temporary variable created only when the method **MyMethod** is called; in this case, it will not be garbage-collected because it is a temporary variable; instead, it will be added to the stack (and consequently deleted from it when the method is exited).

BOXING AND UNBOXING

While the heap and the stack are used for different purposes, there are cases when it may be necessary to convert a value type to a reference type and vice-versa. Let's look at the next example.

```
Class TestPerf
{
    public void test()
    {
        int test = 23;
        Object a = test
//boxing: conversion from stack to heap

        test = (int) a;
//unboxing: converting from heal to stack
    }
}
```

In the previous code:

- We first transfer the value of the variable **tes**t to the variable **a**; this is called **boxing** because the value that was initially saved in the stack (the variable **test** is an integer that is stored in the stack) is now stored in the heap (the variable **a** is an object that is stored in the heap).

- We then transfer the value of the object **a** to the variable **test**; this is called **unboxing** because the value that was initially saved in the heap (the variable **a** is an object that is stored in the heap) is now saved in the stack (the variable **test** is an integer that is stored in the stack).

While it may be tempting to box or unbox variables, this should be reduced to a minimum, as it usually has a cost in terms of performance and memory.

CALLING THE GARBAGE COLLECTOR OFTEN

One of the other tricks that you can use is to employ a small-size heap with frequent garbage collection. In this case, the heap size is small, so the garbage collection should not be too time-consuming; in this case, you could, for example, trigger the GC every 30 frames, as illustrated in the next code example.

```
if (Time.frameCount % 30 == 0)
{
    System.GC.Collect();
}
```

- In the previous code, we check if the frame count is a multiple of 30. If this is the case, then we call the garbage collector.

This method might be especially interesting if you would like to keep a high frame rate for your game.

ALLOCATING AND DEALLOCATING MEMORY

Heap allocation and deallocation are usually time-consuming. And while allocation is managed by you (as you instantiate an object, for example), you have less control over deallocation, which is usually performed by the Garbage Collector. However, the GB process is triggered in specific situations, or when particular conditions are met. So if you can match (or create) these conditions, you can, as a result, indirectly trigger the GB process. You can think about the GC as an automatic hoover that hoovers a room only when some conditions are met. While you can't always command this hoover , you can certainly make sure that some conditions are (e.g., low virtual memory) met in order to either trigger or not trigger this hoover to start its job.

USING AND CONCATENATING STRINGS

If you are concatenating strings, since these are stored in the heap, you may, instead of adding them using the operator **+**, use **System.Text.StringBuilder**. Because strings are "immutable", in other terms, you can't change the content of a string without creating a new string object, you may instead use **StringBuilder**, which represents a mutable string of character. In other words, a string of characters that can be changed overtime. This means that memory will be allocated when the object is created, but no additional allocation will be required as the string is modified (i.e., through concatenation). This is illustrated in the next code snippet

```
using System.Text.

...


string myName = "Hello";

myName += "is Pat";


//Better

StringBuilder myNameStringBuilder = new StringBuilder();

myNameStringBuilder.Append("Hello ");

myNameStringBuilder.Append(" Pat");
```

KEY TIPS TO KEEP YOUR GAME WORKING SMOOTHLY

So as you can see, optimizing your performance can be due to several factors that can be monitored in the **Profiler**. Some of these key factors include: the time to execute a piece of code, how many time it is called, whether variables are created or discarded, and where and how these were initially created (that is, the heap or the stack). Depending on these parameters, and if you keep an eye on your code to ensure that it does not create unnecessary garbage collection, you should be able to boost the speed of your game, or at least, to keep it running at a reliable and consistent frame rate. It takes, of course, a bit of practice and awareness to apply these. However, if you ever felt (and noticed) poor frame rate in your game, or your application slowing down, these are areas that you may consider in order to make your code leaner and faster.

When it comes to applying these principles in Unity, there are a few things that you can do:

- Recycle objects created in the heap (instances) so that the garbage collector is not called as often and so that a **new** statement (to create a new object) is not used.

- Avoid, as much as possible, boxing and unboxing.

- Use local variables when possible (these will be stored in the stack, and not in the heap) and memory management will be faster and easier in this case.

- Use reference allocation (by creating a new object using the **new** keyword) at the start of the application so that they are called once and not repeatedly, as this will impact on the performances of your game.

- If one of your methods returns an array, you can, instead, use a reference instead of returning a new array, especially if this method is called often. The same applies if you return other types of reference types variables.

- Use **System.Text.StringBuilder** if you need to modify strings at run-time

USING COROUTINES.

In a nutshell, coroutines are a bit like a soccer team where the ball is passed to a player; this player receives the ball and starts to run, however, s/he needs information from the team doctor to know whether s/he can go ahead and what s/he can do to heal a recent injury. So s/he just passes the ball to another team mate and freezes (or waits) until s/he receives instructions from the doctor. When s/he receives this instruction, the ball is passed to him/her again and s/he resumes to play. So in this case, the players share the ball, but only one player has the ball at one particular time. So coroutines are a way to collaboratively run a program with only one function running at a time. If you have used threads, coroutines and threads differ in that threads run in parallel whereas coroutines work collaboratively to freeze one function and give it the focus again when criteria have been fulfilled (that is, only one coroutine running at any given time). Coroutines are usually referred as **concurrency** as they pass control to each-other.

A coroutine is interesting in that it can give the control back to the main program and then the coroutine can resume where it stopped. So you can call the coroutine, and have it to complete some work, and give the control back to the main program if need be. So because you can keep track of where the routine paused, it can be useful to schedule events so that the coroutine completes tasks only in specific circumstances.

By default, a coroutine method will always be declared with the keyword **IEnumerator** beforehand. It also usually includes a **yield** statement marking where the coroutine should pause and resume. A coroutine is also usually called using the keyword **StartCoroutine**, as illustrated in the next code snippet.

```
void Update ()
{

    StartCoroutine (myCoRutine ());

}
IEnumerator myCoRutine ()
{


    yield return 0;

}
```

In the previous code;

- We call the method **myCoRoutine** from the **Update** method.

- The method **myCoRoutine** that will be used as a coroutine, is declared with the keyword **IEnumerator**. This makes sure that this method can be paused and resumed as a coroutine where the **yield** keyword appears.

- The coroutine returns directly to the part of the program that called it in the first place.

The only issue with this code is that the coroutine will be called every frame (which defeats the purpose of the coroutine). If instead, we would prefer the coroutine to be called every 5 seconds, we could manage to freeze it for 5 seconds using the method **WaitForSeconds**. This method, as illustrated in the next code snippet, can be used to pause a coroutine for a specific amount of time.

```
float time;
void Start ()
{
      time = 0;
}
void Update ()
{
      time += Time.deltaTime;
      StartCoroutine (myCoRoutine ());
}
IEnumerator myCoRoutine ()
{
      while (time >5)
      {
            time = 0;
            print ("Hello time: "+ (int)time);
            yield return (new WaitForSeconds(5));
            print ("Just resuming after 5 seconds");
      }
}
```

In the previous code:

- We create a variable called **time**, that will be used to monitor the time.

- This variable is increased every seconds.

- As previously, we call the coroutine **myCoRoutine**.

- In this coroutine, we create a loop that will be triggered whenever the time goes over 5 seconds.

- As we enter the loop we reset the time to **0**.

- We also print a message that includes the time and then pause this coroutine for 5 seconds. So the next time the routine resumes (that is, after 5 seconds), it should print the message "**Resuming after 5 seconds**" which is located just after the yield statement.

- The **time** variable will be increased by one every seconds in the meantime. While the coroutine is suspended, the **Update** function is still executed, so the time is updated every seconds.

- So after 5 seconds, the coroutine is resumed, and the value of the variable **time** is also more than 5. This means that we will enter the loop and resume just after the **yield** statement.

- Because the time is reset to 0 every time we enter this loop, and because we are using a **while loop**, the coroutine will indefinitely be called every 5 seconds.

Note that the condition for the coroutine to pause is that 5 seconds have elapsed. This is done through the statement **new WaitForSeconds(5)**. This being said, it is also possible to employ other conditions to specify when the coroutine should resume, such as **WaitUntil** or **WaitWhile**. For example, we could use the following code instead.

```
yield return (new WaitUntil (()=> time>5));
```

In the previous code, we will wait to resume the coroutine until the variable **time** is greater than 5.

So this example shows how you can manage to schedule events and actions that should only be executed at specific times and these actions are embedded in coroutines that can be frozen overtime. To use the analogy of a soccer team: every 5 seconds we pass the ball to the player X (the coroutine) who will perform actions with it (for example, dribble) and will pass the ball back to other members of the team after this time has elapsed.

> Note that we have used a loop in the code; otherwise, we could not indefinitely call the coroutine.

So coroutines are very useful because they make it possible to run code asynchronously and they can be used in several occasions, including:

- Scheduling actions based on time (as we have seen above).

- Loading elements in your game at specific times, to ensure that the game will still be responsive.

- Suspending execution until data has arrived (we will have a look at this in the next section).

- Scheduling the actions of Non-Player Characters over time.

- Customizing any action performed in the **Update** function (including dealing with finite state machines).

Using coroutines is often useful to load data over the internet. The following code could be used to load the content of a PHP page.

```
using UnityEngine;
using System.Collections;


public class AccessDB : MonoBehaviour {
    string url = "http://localhost:8888/updateScore.php";


    // Use this for initialization
    IEnumerator Start()
    {
        WWW www = new WWW(url);
        yield return www;
        string result = www.text;
        print("data received"+result);
    }
    void Update () {


    }
}
```

In the previous code:

- We declare the class **AccessDB**.

- We then create a string called **url** that stores the address of the PHP page that we will access.

- We declare a function called **Start** using the keyword **IEnumerator** beforehand. This keyword is used to specify that the function **Start** has become a coroutine, which means that it now has the ability to be paused until a condition has been fulfilled.

In our case, it is necessary to declare this function as a coroutine because the code that we use to gather information from the PHP script will need to send a request to the server and then wait for the server's answer. However, we don't want the whole program to stop while this data is on its way because we still need to update the screen and perform other important tasks in the meantime. So in that sense, this function does not act like a usual function, in that it doesn't just perform actions and return to where it was called from. Instead, because part of its purpose is to gather (and possibly wait for) information from the server, which may involve delays, as a coroutine, this function will fetch for the server's data and pause itself until the data has been received. Meanwhile, other functions, such as the **Update** function, will be able to run. Then, when the data is received from the server, the **Start** function is called again just after the point where it had been paused.

DELEGATES

A delegate is basically comparable to a container; in the same ways variable hold values, delegates with hold a reference to one or several functions This is very useful if you want to call several methods at the same time, for example.

To be able to use delegates, the following steps are often necessary:

- Define a template for the functions that will be associated with this delegate (for example, their return type and their list of parameters).

- Instantiate a new delegate.

- Associate this new delegate to one or several methods.

Let's look at the following example to understand how delegates can be employed in C#:

```
public class delegatesExample : MonoBehaviour
{

    delegate void DelegateType1 (string message);

    DelegateType1 myDelegate;

    void Start () {

        myDelegate = fn1;myDelegate ("hello");

        myDelegate = fn2;myDelegate ("hello");

    }

    public void fn1 (string string1)

    {

        print (string1+" from fn1");

    }

    public void fn2 (string string1)

    {

        print (string1+" from fn2");

    }

}
```

In the previous code:

- We define a type for our delegate. So based on this definition, any delegate of type **DelegateType1** can be associated with **void** methods that take a **string** parameter.

- We then declare a new delegate called **myDelegate**.

- Once this is done, we instantiate our delegate using both the methods **fn1** and **fn2** that are defined lower down the code snippet.

- You may notice that both methods match the type of the delegate as they don't return values (their return type is **void**) and they take one **string** variable as a parameter.

- The first time this delegate is instantiated, it is associated to the method **fn1**. In other words, calling the delegate will result in calling the method **fn1**.

- The same is done for the method **fn2**.

> So, as you have seen in this example, delegates are comparable to variables in the sense that they are containers, but unlike variables, they refer to methods instead of values.

Now, there are times when you may want to include more than one method in a delegate container so that calling the delegates calls simultaneously several functions instead of one.

This can be done easily by replacing these lines…

```
myDelegate = fn1;myDelegate ("Hello");
myDelegate = fn2;myDelegate ("Hello");
```

…with these lines:

```
myDelegate += fn1; myDelegate += fn2;
myDelegate ("Hello");
```

In the previous code:

- We successively add **fn1** and **fn2** to the delegate.

- We then call the **delegate**.

- As a result, both the messages "**Hello from fn1**" and "**Hello from fn2**" should be printed in the **Console**.

EVENTS AND DELEGATES

As we have seen previously, delegates are very useful when the function to be called may differ depending on specific circumstances. Delegates can also be associated to events so that when the event occurs, a specific function can be called based on specific circumstances, and we will look at this principle in the next paragraphs.

Events are useful as they help to optimize your code. Their principle is simple: you define an event and specify what should be done if this event happens. In our case, a function (or a delegate) could be associated to this event and be called when this event occurs.

Instead of constantly pooling (or looking for) a specific event, you will be notified when this event occurs, and this can save significant time and make your code leaner and more efficient. This concept is comparable to asking your friend to call you when s/he knows that concert tickets are on sale, instead or calling him or her every minute.

We could take the analogy of a calendar. You could look at a specific website every day to check whether there will be high temperatures tomorrow, or instead, subscribe to an alert service that will let you know automatically when predicted temperatures are high.

To apply the concept of delegate and events, you will usually need do the following:

- Declare a delegate type.

- Declare an event of the type defined above.

- Make sure that the event can be accessed from outside the class without having to instantiate the class.

- Register this event with any other script that needs to know when this event is happening.

- Define what needs to be done in the previous script in case a notification has been sent and received.

To implement this concept, we could, for example, create a script called **MyEventManager**, as illustrated in the next code snippet, and link it to an empty object.

```
public class MyEventManager : MonoBehaviour
{

    public delegate void DelegateType1 (string name);

    public static event DelegateType1 keyTyped;

    void Update ()
    {

        if (Input.GetKeyDown (KeyCode.A))
        {

            keyTyped ("A");

        }

    }

}
```

In the previous code:

- We declare a class called **MyEventManager**.

- We then declare a delegate type called **DelegateType1**.

- We declare an event called **keyTyped** of type **DelegateType1**. Note that an event is a special type of delegate that includes added security features that make them more appropriate for this purpose. This being said, we could have used a delegate instead.

- We detect when the player presses the key **A**. In this case the event (or delegate) called **keyTyped** is called.

- If you remember well, based on the delegate type, we pass a string as a parameter;

So, at this stage, we have defined the delegate that should be called when the key **A** is called. The next step is to make sure that the scripts interested in this event subscribe to this event. We also need to define what these scripts should do when this event occurs and when they are notified accordingly.

This could be done by creating the following script.

```
public class EventSubscriber : MonoBehaviour
{

    void OnEnable()

    {

        MyEventManager.keyTyped += doSomething;

    }

    void Disable()

    {

        MyEventManager.keyTyped -= doSomething;

    }

    void doSomething (string fname)

    {

        print ("You pressed" + fname);

    }

}
```

In the previous code:

- We declare a new class called **EventSubscriber**.

- We use the methods **OnEnable** and **OnDisable**.

- In the method **OnEnable**, that is called whenever the object linked to this script is active and/or enabled, we specify that we subscribe to the event **keyTyped**, and that in case it happens, we should call the method **doSomething**.

- In the method **OnDisable**, that is called whenever the object linked to this script is deleted and/or deactivated, we specify that we unsubscribe to the event **keyTyped**, and that in case this event happens we should not do anything.

- The methods **OnEnable** and **OnDisable** are chosen here, essentially for safety because they are called after the methods **Awake** but before the method **Start**.

While Unity provides simple ways to deal with events and notifications using UnityEvents (please see the section on *drag and drop*), it is always a good idea to understand how events and delegates work, as they are the building blocks of UnityEvents.

SETTING UP AND MANAGING YOUR GAME

One of the key issues, when you create your game, is to find a way to manage all its parts and to access important information at all times.

Because, by default, most of your objects will be destroyed once a new scene is created, it is necessary to create a game manager that will persist over the entire course of the game.

This game manager would have the responsibility to: initialize and load levels, keep track of where the user is in the game (for example, the current scene, the current menu or the current level.

One very simple way to achieve this, is to create an empty object, that is associated to a script that specifies that the linked object should not be destroyed every time we load a new scene.

It could be implemented this way:

```
public class MyGameManager : MonoBehaviour
{
    int nbLives = 0;
    int startingLevel = 0;


    void Awake ()
    {
        DontDestroyOnLoad (gameObject.transform);
    }
}
```

In the previous code:

* We several variables that will be used throughout the game.

* Using the **Awake** function, that is called once in the lifetime of the game, we specify that the GameObject linked to this script should not be destroyed.

* You can then perform several other initializations in the same script related to background audio, or the level to be loaded. So this object will be helping to synchronize the loading of the different elements of your game.

CREATING MAINTAINABLE AND REUSABLE CODE

When you are coding your game, the size and structure of your code can rapidly become overwhelming over time, unless you have, from the beginning, set a defined strategy that you will follow to ensure that your code will grow in a way that is manageable. To achieve this goal, there are several ways that you can follow including a component-based structure.

In Unity, most of the games that you will create, by default, will follow a component-based approach, which is essentially how scenes and objects are created in Unity. Unity is using a component-based architecture where each **GameObject** can include one or more components, which can, in turn be made of or manage other components.

A component often has a specific functionality and purpose. For example, a component can be used for collision detection (for example, **BoxCollider**), to render a **GameObject** (for example, **Mesh Renderer**) or to add physics properties (for example, **RigidBody**) to a **GameObject**. Each component will work regardless of the GameObject it is attached to. In addition, components can also communicate between them to exchange information.

Each of the components' properties can be seen in the **Inspector**, which makes it easier to add or modify a component and to then see how it impacts on the game. Since adding or amending a component can be done very quickly in Unity (for example, using drag and drop), the component structure makes sense in Unity as it speeds up the way you can test your ideas.

This being said, it can be argued that, on the long run, with rather complex and large projects, this approach may not be suitable, and you may instead change your approach to a stricter Object-Oriented structure. There is no right or wrong approach but instead an approach that matches your progression or stage.

For this section, we will essentially focus on a component-based structure to match Unity's way of doing things. However, you can if you wish look for additional resources on OOP structures, for your information.

So, to create your games in Unity, and if you are coming from an Object-Oriented background, you may need to think in terms of components, in the sense that you may need to start creating small scripts that implement a specific feature but that are not tied to a particular object or class. Ideally a component should know nothing about the GameObject it is attached to. This makes your component more modular and it also makes it possible to build a game that is truly component-based and hence, modular.

In a component-based architecture, all **GameObjects** will share some features (that is, components) such as a **Renderer** or a **Collider**, for example. However, the number and types of components for a particular object makes this **GameObject** unique.

Using a component-based approach has, of course its challenges. One of these challenges is linked to communication and synchronization between these components, especially when one component is waiting for another component to perform a particular task. In this case, thankfully, Unity provides the class **SendMessage**. Using this class, a GameObject can send messages to all of its components and exclusively target the components that are interested in that message. This can be achieved using the option **SendMessageOptions.RequireReceiver**.

For example, if you plan to create NPCs with different behaviours, you could do the following:

- Start to evaluate the features or "abilities" that the NPC will require. For example, the NPC may need to navigate, sense the presence of the player, include a finite state machine, have a weapon inventory system, have an appearance, have intelligence, be able to attack, be able to chase the player, or be able to look for ammunitions when needed.

- You can then identify existing components provided by Unity that may be able to fulfill some of these features (for example, *Renderer*, or *Navmesh Agent*).

- Implement the components that don't exist yet (for example, vision, hearing, or inventory) using your own scripts.

- You can then create different types of NPCs that consist of a combination of these components.

Let's look at the example of an NPC:

When creating NPCs in our game, we could, for example, define the following components:

- Health: to manage health levels and to be able to increase or decrease health accordingly.

- Navigation: this can be managed with a NavMesh Agent.

- Intelligence: this can be managed by the Animator Controller (that is, a finite state machine).

- Smell: this will give our NPC a sense of smell based on distance. This can be implemented based on distance in a script that we could create.

- Hearing: this will give our NPC the ability to hear. This can be implemented based on distance in a script that we could create.

- WeaponManagement: this will make it possible for the NPC to manage weapons and can be implemented in a script that we could create.

- Weapons: these will be managed by the WeaponManagement component defined previously.

- Lead: this could be added later-on so that an NPC has the ability to lead a particular group of NPCs.

All components can of course include their own variables and methods and communicate between each other using the syntax **SendMessage, including** to notify relevant components of the occurrence of specific events.

ADVANCED PROGRAMMING WITH C# PATTERNS

Although this book will not cover C# patterns, as there are books out there that do a great job at explaining what they are, it may be a good idea, for your own development to look at how design patterns may help you to structure your code. These are solutions to common problems encountered by developers in terms of code architecture or optimization

As we have considered some general techniques to optimize your code, the following will describe additional considerations and options that you may use to boost the performances of your game based on its structure. While these techniques are not covered in-depth in this book, knowing about them is always an advantage. Many of these concepts are based on common design patters, which are reusable solutions to problem commonly found in software development. So the following sections will provide you with ideas and concepts that could be useful when you develop your game.

As you read these patterns, you will probably discover that you have already implemented some of them by using and combining some of the code structures and examples already provided in this book.

WHAT ARE DESIGN PATTERNS?

As mentioned earlier, *design patterns* are reusable solutions to problem commonly found in software. These solutions, that are addressed by *design patterns*, are often linked to key issues experienced by software engineers, including software maintainability, software interaction with users, and memory management. As a result, design patterns can be of different types including: creational design patterns (to instantiate classes), structural design patterns (that is, how classes and objects are organized), and behavioral design patterns (that is, how classes and objects communicate between them).

Now, for the purpose of this book, we will only focus on some of the key patterns that you could use in games, including: **Model-View-Controller**, **Singleton**, **Observer**, **and State**. The next sections will briefly describe each of these and how they may be implemented.

MODEL-VIEW CONTROLLER (MVC) PATTERN

In this pattern, an application (in our case a game) is viewed as (or divided in) three components: The **M**odel or world simulation (for example, game rules and mechanics), the **V**iew world visualization (the game's visual representation), and the **C**ontroller (that is, the interaction with the player). So for example, whenever the player interacts with the game through a controller or the keyboard (that is, the **Controller**), the **Model** is updated (for example, the score or the coordinates or of the character are updated), and the **View** is updated (that is, the scene is rendered and the player's representation is visibly different on screen).

STATE PATTERN

In the **State** pattern, an object's behaviors will differ depending on its current state. This can be used in different ways for a game, including: menus that correspond to different states in the game (for example, the splash screen, the briefing section, or during game-play), or Artificial Intelligence (for example, the NPC can be idle, walking, or running).

These states have the advantage of providing more control of and visibility in the flow of the game. For example, it is easy to know what states we are in and to modify the game accordingly, since the NPC is in only one state at any given time.

In terms of resources management, it is also more efficient because resources necessary for a particular state can be loaded during the transition to this state. In Unity, you can use a **Finite-State-Machine** where states are defined and transitions between these states occur when specific conditions have been fulfilled.

It can be used especially when animating characters, or for general AI behaviors. One of the drawbacks of this pattern is that it may be impossible to access two states at the same time (for example, playing the game and accessing the help menu that was initially declared as a different state). The state pattern can also be illustrated, to some extent, by the use of coroutines. As we have seen earlier, when accessing a database, some functions may be called from the main part of the game, but may also need to wait for data before they return control to the main part of the game. However, you can foresee that if it takes a while to obtain this information, your game could be virtually frozen until the data has been acquired. So, to get around this issue, you can use coroutines. These will basically pause their execution until a condition has been met, but return control to the part of the code that called it in the first place, and resume the code within the function only when the condition has been fulfilled (for example, when the data has been received).

SINGLETON PATTERN

In the **Singleton** pattern, a class can only have one instance. This pattern has many advantages, but can also lead to issues when misused. A singleton is a class that allows only one instance to be created. In theory, you would not use it often, but there are times when it may be needed specifically for database access, a game manager, a game inventory, or anything in your game that only needs to be instantiated once. Singletons can then be associated to delegates in order to manage events.

OBSERVER PATTERN

In the **Observer** pattern, an object is notified when the status or states of other objects have changed. This concept is, for example, used for events and delegates. The idea of events is that a class is notified when an event has occurred without having to look for this data continuously, and hence saving you a lot of time and resources. Using delegates, you can also optimize events based on several conditions. For example, when an event occurs (for example, after 120 seconds), you can create an event and decide to call specific functions accordingly. For example, at the start of the game, you can create NPCs with low intelligence. As the game and time progress, NPCs of increasing intelligence can be created. Again, there is no need to pool (wait) for the time in this situation. Instead, you can create events and associate them to functions called when this events occurs.

OBJECT POOLING

The **Object Pooling** pattern is concerned with boosting performance by reducing the number of instantiations, when the cost of initializing a class is high. So objects are being reused. This being said, because it would alter performances to wait for an object to be released, this pattern also accounts for creating new objects when needed, but to also to clean-up (and pool) objects, that are not used, on a regular basis.

Often, when you create a game where NPCs can be neutralized, the corresponding objects are usually destroyed. However, there is usually a cost associated to creating or destroying an object, in terms of memory, as we have seen earlier. So this could be improved by recycling objects instead of recreating them. This concept is called *object pooling* and is especially useful when multiple instances of an object are used in a scene

For example, several bullets per seconds can be destroyed a few seconds after they have been created in a First-Person shooter. Using object pooling, we could instead reuse bullets instead of destroying them.

MORE ABOUT DESIGN PATTERNS

This section has given you an overview of design patterns that you can use in your game; you may already have used some of these without even realizing it, for example, when you have created delegates, a state machine, or coroutines.

If you would like to know more about design patterns, you may check the following resources:

- The book "Game Programming Patterns" from Robert Nystrom does a very good job at it, and you may check his online resources here.

- C# Design Patterns: a collection C# patterns.

LEVEL ROUNDUP

Summary

In this chapter, we have managed to look at ways to improve your code and the performance of your game, including memory management. Along the way, we have also learned about useful structures such as delegates, scriptable objects, or coroutines. So well done! This is quite a significant leap from the last chapter.

Quiz

Now, let's check your knowledge! Please answer the following questions (the answers are included in the resource pack) or specify whether they are correct or incorrect.

1. Empty magic and overridable methods such as Start or Update still cost resources as they are called at run-time

2. It's ok to use search functions such as **GameObject.Find** in the Update method.

3. Public variables cannot be hidden from the Inspector.

4. It is good practice **<u>NOT</u>** to include computer intensive code in the methods **Update** and **FixedUpdate**.

5. A script attached to an object, but deactivated will have no impact on performance.

6. An empty overridable (or magic) function, will have no impact on the performance of the game.

7. It is a good idea to use the method **GameObject.Find** in the **Update** function to increase performance.

8. A coroutine can be paused.

9. Design patterns make it possible to optimize your code and to also answer common problems faced by developers.

10. Unity uses a component-based approach.

Quiz Solution

Now, let's check your knowledge!

1. True.

2. False.

3. False.

4. True.

5. True.

6. False.

7. False.

8. True.

9. True.

10. True.

6

FREQUENTLY ASKED QUESTIONS

This chapter provides answers to the most frequently asked questions about the features that we have covered in this book. Please also note that some <u>videos are also available on the companion site</u> to help you with some of the concepts covered in this book.

C# SCRIPTS

How do I create a script?

In the **Project** window, select: **Create | C# Script**.

How can my script be executed?

Your C# script may need to be attached to an object. This being said, you could also create a class that is not linked to an object but that is used indirectly by another class (that is, instantiated).

How can I check that my script has no errors?

Open the **Console** window and any error should be displayed there.

What is object-oriented programming?

In object-oriented programming, your program is seen as a collection of objects that interact with each other using, for example, methods.

Should the name of my C# file and the containing class within be the same?

When you create a new C# file, Unity will let you rename it immediately. Once this is done, Unity will automatically generate the name of the class within, using the name that you have specified for this file. So, if you happened to change the name of this file later on, you may also need to change the name of the class within the file.

Why should I use C#?

There are several good reasons to start coding in C#. One of them is that C# is an object-oriented programming language that is relatively similar to other languages such as Java. So by learning C# you should be able to transfer this knowledge to other languages easily.

What is the dot notation for?

The dot notation refers to **object-oriented programming**. Using dots, you can access properties and functions (or methods) related to a particular object. For example **gameObject.transform.position** gives you access to the **position** from the **transform** of the object linked to a script. It is often useful to read it backward. In this case, the dot can be interpreted as **"of"**. So in our case, **gameObject.transform.position** can be translated as "the position **of** the transform **of** the **gameObject**".

OPTIMIZATION

Why should I optimize my game?

Optimizing your code can make a great difference in the way your game is perceived (and appreciated) by the players. By minimizing bottlenecks and increasing the speed of the game, you can make sure that the player will have a smooth experience.

What can I do to identify bottlenecks in my game?

The first port of call is the **Profiler**, as it will identify methods (and the code) that may use too many resources (for example, execution time or garbage collection).

How can I reduce bottlenecks in my code?

Some of the best things that you can do to make sure that your game will run smoothly include: decreasing garbage collection, reducing computer-intensive code for methods that are called often, reducing the number of instantiations, making sure that empty magic methods are deleted, making sure that scripts are not added twice to an object, and avoiding boxing and unboxing as much as possible.

What are the main differences between the heap and the stack?

The stack is used for local variables. It is relatively fast to access and its memory management is rather simple. The stack is used for classes and objects. Its memory management is slightly more complex and helped by the garage collector. Accessing the heap is relatively slower than the stack.

DETECTING USER INPUTS

How can I detect users' inputs?

In Unity, you can detect several types of inputs including keystrokes, mouse movement, drag and drop, and taps for mobile devices. For more information on these, see the sections called **Combining C# and Unity Objects**.

How can I detect objects in front of the player or the NPC?

You can detect objects using collision detection (based on colliders), triggers (based on a specific area) or using ray-casting. For more information on these, see the sections called **Combining C# and Unity Objects.**

Can I open files from Unity?

Yes, using C# in Unity, you can open or execute files from outside your project (for example, PHP files or XML files) or files that have been imported in your project such as pictures, text files, or audio. You can also use, alternatively, scriptable objects to save and access data at run time. For more information on these, see the sections called **Combining C# and Unity Objects.**

7
THANK YOU

I would like to thank you for completing this book. I trust that you feel proficient in C# now. This book is the second in the series "Unity from Proficiency to Mastery" that covers particular aspects of Unity, so it may be time to move on to the next books where you will get started with even more specific features. You can find a description of these forthcoming books on the official page **http://www.learntocreategames.com/books/**.

In case you have not seen it yet, you can subscribe to our Facebook group using the following link. It includes a community of like-minded game developers who share ideas and are ready to help you with your game projects.

http://facebook.com/groups/learntocreategames/

You may also subscribe to our mailing list to receive weekly updates and information on how to create games and improve your skills.

http://learntocreategames.com/subscribe/

So that the book can be constantly improved, I would really appreciate your feedback. So, please leave me a helpful review on Amazon letting me know what you thought of the book and also send me an email (learntocreategames@gmail.com) with any suggestions you may have. I read and reply to every email.

Thanks so much!!

Thank you

52530241R00170

Made in the USA
Middletown, DE
19 November 2017